Uprooted

by

H.N James

Contents

Preface

As an admirer of the scientific process and the discoveries of the great scientific minds of the past and present, I have come to view the world in a more objective manner, relying upon reason and evidence-based data to reach my own conclusions. I initially compiled the information in this book for my own edification, but have decided to share it with a wider audience in the hopes that others may find my transformation helpful on their own path of discovery.

I have gathered the information for this book over several years from various online documentaries, articles, and scientific journals. Because the scientific community constantly reevaluates its claims, I cannot guarantee this information to be 100% accurate at the time of each individual's reading. In fact, I highly encourage you to conduct your own research and explore the truth for yourself. I simply wish to share this information with you as a starting point for your journey.

The last section of this book titled "Supernova," is a brief autobiography. I included it because of the encouragement of many of my friends suggesting that it would be valuable for the readers to connect to my message. It has no affect on the content of the book, so you can choose to read it at the beginning or the end.

Introduction

The state of mind of a modern human being is quite complex. It is often directed toward preservation of the self, since societal pressures blind us to the damage we inflict upon one another and the other species that share this planet. Because the majority of humanity is largely unaware that the universe itself is the reason for our existence, we live as though we are not part of Earth's amazing bio-diversity and as though we do not play a key role in the pollution and destruction of our own planet.

Social divisions such as financial status and religious views have further physically and mentally detached us from the natural world, as well as desensitized us to the fact that we are all accountable for the evils of our species: war, poverty, famine, and unjustifiable suffering. Humanity's true origins have been glossed over by the belief in a supernatural entity who supposedly created and placed human beings on Earth in order to test their moral fiber. In a system driven by greed and selfish motivation, and with a world population of roughly 7.8 billion, human worth has now become irrelevant and the unique attributes of cooperation, compassion, curiosity, and empathy have become stifled. The artists, scientists, philosophers, and explorers within all of us have been sacrificed to support a self-serving social structure that brings out the worst of humanity.

Yet, I believe that we are capable of overcoming this malicious and destructive cycle with a positive attitude and accurate information about the world in which we belong. We must come to understand the social system we are born into, as well as the natural world that we are indeed a part of—only then can we begin to understand who we are and the role we play in this world.

To understand is to awaken, and to awaken is to escape the toxic constraints of society in order to regain power as a living entity in a universe that has existed for 13.8 billion years. We truly are an incredible species, and we need to learn about our true origins through science in order to realize our true human potential. We must cleanse our consciousness from the damaging, false concepts shaped by society and reawaken the true values that genuinely make us human.

Timeline of Evolutionary Events

In order to appreciate the enormity of the timespan over which our universe, planet, and species evolved, a timeline is included with the following abbreviations:

Ga= billion years ago   **Ma**= million years ago

13.8 Ga	The Big Bang marks the beginning of space and time
13.6 Ga	First instances of light in the universe
12.6 Ga	Formation of the Milky Way galaxy
5 Ga	Formation of our sun
4.6 Ga	Formation of Earth
4.5 Ga	Theia collides with Earth
3.9 Ga	The Late Heavy Bombardment Period
3.8 Ga	First instances of microscopic life on Earth
3.5 Ga	Photosynthetic bacteria emerge
2.1 Ga	Eukaryotic cells begin their evolution
640 Ma	Snowball Earth lasts 50 million years
600 Ma	Complex multi-cellular life forms arise
541 Ma	The Cambrian Explosion produces a great diversification of life
444 Ma	Ordovician- Silurian mass extinction
450-435 Ma	Plants begin to appear on land
376 Ma	Devonian mass extinction

375 Ma	Vertebrates begin to migrate from water to land
320-310 Ma	First reptiles evolve from amphibians
252 Ma	End-Permian mass extinction
230 Ma	First dinosaurs appear
201 Ma	Triassic-Jurassic mass extinction
200 Ma	First mammals appear
65 Ma	Cretaceous-Paleogene mass extinction caused by an asteroid impact
65-55 Ma	Primates evolve
7 Ma	Hominids walk upright
3.3 Ma	Period during which Salam and Lucy lived (*Australopithecus afarensis*)
2.4-1.5 Ma	*Homo habilis* appears
2 Ma	*Homo erectus* evolves
430,000 years ago	*Homo neanderthalensis* appear in Europe
200,000 years ago	*Homo sapiens* evolve from *Homo heidelbergensis* in the Great Rift Valley of eastern Africa
60,000 years ago	*Homo sapiens* begin migrating out of Africa
10,000 years ago	Humans develop agricultural practices

CHAPTER ONE

THE UNIVERSE

The Universe

It is a simple, yet simultaneously complicated fact that we exist on a planet orbiting *one* of hundreds of billions of stars in a vast galaxy that is but *one* of hundreds of billions of galaxies in the universe. Whether we understand or even take an interest in the nature of the universe does not change the fact that we all live within it, and without it, our very existence would not be possible.

To understand our place here, we must first accept the fact that every one of us makes up a part of the universe. We must also learn how it functions and what led to our presence here, because the more we understand the enormity and beauty of our vast cosmos, the wider our perspective becomes, and the more significant our presence in this life will be. The most logical search for answers to explain our existence begins with studying the origin of the universe, since it provides us with an essential understanding of who we are and where we come from. Our current knowledge of the universe is due to the contributions of countless great minds over many centuries, as well as the technological advancements of recent decades.

How We Came to Know the Universe

As our early ancestors became more and more conscious of their surroundings, they began to wonder about the laws of nature that governed them. Witnessing natural phenomena that they could not explain pushed early humans to question their relationship with these events. The beliefs they formed were not necessarily factual, but did serve to offer comfort and security in the face of confusion and fear.

Nearly all ancient cultures began their inquiry into the universe by observing the sky above, with the sun as the focal point of the sky during the day and the moon and stars as the dominant forces of the night. They considered these celestial objects to be deities, and believed that the sun, moon, stars, and planets controlled the lives and fates of the people below.

For thousands of years, our ancestors observed the sky, and once mankind's architectural skills progressed to a more advanced level, we began to build structures that mirrored the heavens and reflected our comprehension of the universe. The oldest such structure, known as the Goseck circle, which consists of four concentric discs, was used to track the course of the sun throughout the different seasons. Discovered in Germany, the Goseck circle dates back to 4900 BCE and is considered to be the first solar observatory. However, the most revolutionary astronomical discovery of our ancient world took place in Mesopotamia, close to modern-day Iraq. It is believed that the ancient civilization of Sumer developed one of the first written languages—cuneiform—around 3500-3000 BCE. Over the next thousand years, priests used this new skill to record the movements of the sun, moon, and stars on clay tablets.

The Babylonian Civilization of 1900 BCE inherited the knowledge of the Sumerians, and their advanced comprehension of mathematics allowed them to accurately record and predict the movement of celestial bodies. The oldest astronomical document is the Venus tablet of Ammisaduqa, dating back to the mid-seventeenth century BCE. It details the movement of Venus across the night sky and is the earliest known instance of a written record of planetary motion.

The Sumerian and Babylonian discoveries in ancient Mesopotamia also served to lay the foundation for Western astronomy, beginning with the ancient Greeks. They relied on complex mathematical calculations to observe the heavens, which enabled them to distinguish between stars and planets using only the naked eye. The Greeks discovered five planets and named them after their gods, but in a tribute to their own deities, the Romans changed the names to those we recognize today: Mercury, Venus, Mars, Jupiter, and Saturn. Greek astronomers believed that Earth was the immobile center of the universe and that all other celestial bodies revolved around it, a theory that demonstrated our own sense of importance and reinforced the idea that human beings had a special relationship with the heavens. In the fourth century BCE, Aristotle speculated that all planets were distant, perfectly smooth orbs composed of materials different from those found on Earth. He also theorized that the stars and other celestial bodies held fixed positions and that the entire cosmos was enclosed in a giant crystalline sphere.

During the second century CE, the Roman astronomer Ptolemy created a complex geocentric model of the planets using epicycles to predict their movements. With this theoretical method, he predicted not only the positions of the planets, but also their relative velocities. Despite the accuracy of his calculations, his model of the universe—with an immobile Earth resting at its center—remained flawed. This became the accepted model of the universe for hundreds of years, since European astronomical advances came to a halt with the defragmentation of the Roman Empire in 476 CE.

It was not until the 15th century that astronomers once again turned their attention to revising their model of the universe. This time, Nicolaus Copernicus, a church deacon and devout Polish Christian, proposed a heliocentric model of the universe. In his book, *De revolutionibus orbium coelestium (On the Revolutions of the Heavenly Spheres)*, Copernicus theorized that rather than being an immobile center of the universe, the Earth was third in a series of planets orbiting the sun. He based his reasoning on a system of circular orbits calculated by noting the trajectories of other planets. Copernicus was also the first to propose that Earth rotated on its own axis once every 24 hours. Fearing reprisal from the Roman Catholic Church for "heretical ideas," Copernicus published his theory just before his death in 1543, and considering the example of Giordano Bruno, he may have been prudent in doing so. Bruno, an Italian philosopher and supporter of Copernicus' ideas, was regarded by his colleagues as a brilliant thinker ahead of his time. He theorized that since our planet revolved around the sun—a star—then the rest of our universe must contain similar stars orbited by other celestial bodies. These statements directly conflicted with the teachings of the Catholic Church, and subsequently led to Bruno's imprisonment in 1593 during the Roman Inquisition. He was found guilty of heresy and burned at the stake in a Roman market square on February 17, 1600.

The next major astronomical discovery came from German mathematician Johannes Kepler, born in 1571. Kepler improved upon the heliocentric model of Copernicus by calculating that planets revolved around the sun in ellipses rather than perfect circles. He noted that the planets did not travel at constant rates, as previously believed, but increased their speed as they approached the sun and slowed down as they moved further away from it. Kepler published these mathematical observations in *Astronomia Nova* (*A New Astronomy*) in 1609, but his book drew little attention, since many scientists were unwilling to accept a model of the universe with the sun at its center because they feared persecution from the Catholic Church.

The spring of 1609 brought the Dutch "spy glass" to shops across Europe, and Galileo Galilei, an Italian mathematician, astronomer, engineer, and physicist modified this new invention to substantiate the theories of Copernicus and Kepler. Originally meant for nautical navigation, Galileo recognized the spy glass' potential for celestial observation and improved upon the original model to magnify images to the power of 30. In November of that same year, Galileo turned his telescope toward the heavens and began to record his observations. This was truly a monumental event in history, as he discovered not only thousands of stars, but also craters and mountains on the surface of the Earth's moon. He observed multiple moons circling Jupiter and concluded that Venus also orbits the sun by comparing its moon phases with those of the Earth's. The widely-held perception of the Earth resting at the center of the universe had begun to shatter.

As previously described by ancient Greek philosophers, the Catholic Church maintained that all celestial bodies, perfectly spherical and uniform, revolved around the Earth. In 1610, Galileo published his observations of the sky in *Sidereus Nuncius (Starry Messenger)*, which supported Copernicus' heliocentric model of the universe. Galileo later travelled to Rome to spread his ideas about the Copernican system, often encouraging others to observe the sky through his telescope in order to see and understand his theories for themselves. Despite this candid approach, Pope Paul V quickly condemned these ideas, as they contradicted the Bible and the teachings of the Catholic Church, particularly the belief that God created the Earth and placed it in the center of our cosmos.

In March 1616, the Roman Catholic Church prohibited the publication of any heliocentric works, and even removed *Starry Messenger* from circulation. In a bizarre twist, the book was finally recirculated in 1620 after the omission of nine sentences. The Church forbade Galileo from publicly discussing the sun as the center of the universe, lest he be charged with heresy and put to death.

The year 1623 saw a close friend of Galileo's inaugurated as Pope Urban VIII, and believing he now possessed a supporter at the head of the church, he wrote *Dialogue Concerning the Two Chief World Systems*, which both defended the Copernican model of the universe and mocked the Catholic Church. Ten years later, Pope Urban VIII summoned Galileo to stand trial on counts of heresy. He was found guilty and ordered to publically repudiate his theories or be persecuted to the fullest extent of the law. Galileo denied his own teachings in order to avoid a gruesome death, and served a sentence of house arrest for the remainder of his life, forbidden from discussing or studying astronomy.

We can only wonder how much more rapidly our collective scientific knowledge might have developed if the Catholic Church had not interfered with the work of so many of astronomy's pioneering intellectuals. For more than 200 years, this powerful religious body stood in the way of one of the most significant discoveries of modern astronomy, despite the fact that this model would later be recognized as the foundation of the Scientific Revolution. The Catholic Church's prohibition on publishing heliocentric works continued until 1758, and the printing of new scientific theories was only allowed later in 1822. Were it not for the works of Copernicus, Kepler, and Galileo, we would not have been able to develop the many technologies we rely on today, yet the Catholic Church vehemently denied each of these men's theories and threatened their lives.

In 1643, one year after Galileo's death, English mathematician and physicist Isaac Newton was born. With his own observations and calculations, as well as the findings of preceding geniuses, Newton published one of the first significant works of the Enlightenment, which demonstrated that the universe is subject to certain indisputable laws of nature. By shining a beam of white light through a prism, he showed that light disperses into all colors found in the visible spectrum, which later allowed scientists to understand the composition of planetary atmospheres and stars, as well as the rotation rates of planets.

In 1668, nearly 60 years after Galileo invented the first telescope to observe the night sky, Newton developed an improved version with a revolutionary method of collecting and focusing light, a creation known today as the Newtonian telescope. A small convex mirror reflects and focuses light onto a second flat mirror, which then bounces the beam of light onto lenses inside the tube. This new design helped prevent perceived images and colors from blurring, a problematic feature of earlier refracting telescopes.

Using Kepler's laws of planetary motion to substantiate the heliocentric model of the universe, Newton published his revolutionary work, *Philosophiæ Naturalis Principia Mathematica* (*Mathematical Principles of Natural Philosophy*) in 1687. He explained the mysterious mechanisms governing the motions of the planets and objects on Earth and the theory of gravity was born. Newton deduced that any falling object was in fact pulled toward a second object, and demonstrated that the moon was attracted to the Earth, the oceans were attracted to the moon (tidal fluctuations), and that both the Earth and the moon were attracted to the sun. He further demonstrated that the closer one object was to another, the stronger the gravitational pull between these two objects.

In 1781, William Herschel, a classically-trained English musician-turned-astronomer, discovered Uranus, the first planet to be identified in more than 3,500 years. In light of this finding, King George III of England appointed him to court astronomer the following year. During this engagement, Herschel constructed several telescopes and set out to meticulously survey the night sky. He recorded all the new stars and celestial bodies he could see, including thousands of hazy white objects called nebulas. Herschel confirmed that our solar system was part of the Milky Way, a galaxy much larger than previously assumed, and in 1783, he discovered that even the sun did not hold a permanently fixed position, but also moved through space. With a basic understanding of our place in the galaxy, astronomers began to wonder about the nature of stars as well as the vast distances that separated them.

The 19th century revolutionized our understanding of the cosmos thanks to two significant developments in spectroscopy and photography. In 1814, Joseph von Fraunhofer, a German optician, invented the spectroscope, a device which analyzes the color of the light emitted by a heated gas in order to identify its chemical composition. When an element is heated to extremely high temperatures, it emits a unique wavelength, somewhat like an atomic finger print, which scientists could now use to identify the elemental composition of any celestial body. The second great advancement came nearly 25 years later in France, when artist and photographer Louis Daguerre introduced the first practical camera, which astronomers later mounted to a telescope.

In 1838, German astronomer Friedrich Bessel became the first person to measure the distance between the sun and another star using the parallax method, which allowed scientists to determine a star's brightness compared to that of the sun. Several months after Bessel's death in 1846, his colleague Johann Gottfried Galle relied on French astronomer Urbain Le Verrier's calculations for his discovery of Neptune, and our modern solar system was complete.

In 1859, German chemist Robert Bunsen and physicist Gustav Kirchhoff created their own spectroscope, allowing them to identify sodium, lithium, and potassium. They also discovered cesium in 1860 and rubidium the following year. The spectroscope enabled Bunsen and Kirchhoff to observe the light spectrum of the sun and determine it was composed of the same hydrogen atoms found on Earth. In 1861, English astronomer William Huggins detected the atomic composition of stars by combining a spectroscope with a telescope. He discovered that the same elements identified in the sun by Bunsen and

Kirchhoff were also present in other stars, thus confirming that our sun was composed of the same elements as any other star in the universe.

The 20th century brought with it countless technological advancements that aided our astronomical inquiry. Powerful telescopes allowed us to look deeper into the mysterious universe than ever before, and supercomputers permitted researchers to receive and process data at dizzying rates. This progress would not have been possible without the accomplishments of those previously mentioned, but in 1905, one of the most famous and influential minds of the scientific community, Albert Einstein, initiated a revolution in physics that would forever change our views of the universe.

In his theory of special relativity, Einstein studied the three dimensions of space and the singular dimension of time. Previously conceived as separate entities, Einstein wove them into one continuous fabric known as the space-time continuum. From his discovery of the velocity of light, Einstein introduced $E = MC^2$, demonstrating that energy and matter are interchangeable. In 1915, he redefined gravity in his gravitational field equations of general relativity, proving that the weight of heavy objects such as stars and planets warps the fabric of space-time. This established the fact that the sun does not pull the Earth toward it, but instead distorts the fabric of space-time, pushing the Earth toward the sun. In

1921, Einstein received the Nobel Prize in Physics for his theories, many of which would later pave the way for a deeper understanding of the origin of the universe.

In 1918, the American astronomer Harlow Shapley used standard candles to estimate the distance from our solar system to the center of our galaxy. Standard candles are a class of stars with a known brightness, and by comparing their brightness to the total amount of energy they emit, astronomers can approximate the distance to these stars using the inverse square law equation. Shapley calculated the sun to be 30,000 light years from the center of our galaxy, which turned out to be quite close to the accepted distance of 27,000 light years, a truly monumental discovery that once again redefined our place in the cosmos—neither Earth nor the sun rested at the center of the universe, but that its midpoint was actually a great distance from our planet. Until this point in time, we believed that our Milky Way represented the finite universe, but one American astronomer's work would soon destroy this notion.

In 1919, Edwin Hubble began his work at the Mount Wilson Observatory in Los Angeles, California, using the largest and most sophisticated telescope of the time. He detected the fuzzy spiral nebulas thought to be star clusters inside the Milky Way and used the standard candle method to determine the distance between them. Over the course of a year and a half, Hubble calculated a particular star in the

Andromeda nebula to be one million light years away from the Milky Way, and thus in a separate galaxy altogether. Hubble determined that this and similar nebulas were actually distant galaxies, and this shocking discovery confirmed that the universe is billions of light years wide and home to billions of galaxies containing billions of stars.

As Hubble was observing the Milky Way, a Belgian Catholic priest named Georges Lemaître contended that there was a distinct moment in time when the universe came into existence. Applying Einstein's theory of general relativity, Lemaître theorized that if the universe were static, the mass of its matter would be affected by gravity, causing it to cluster together. Since this was not the case, he deduced that the universe was expanding, and proposed that at one point it must have been a dense atom until it exploded. In 1927, Lemaître coined the term "hypothesis of the primeval atom," which we now refer to as the Big Bang theory.

In 1929, after years of careful observation, Hubble realized that different galaxies were slowly moving away from one another. With the spectroscope, scientists can detect an object's motion in relation to the vantage point to determine its speed, as well as the direction it is moving. For example, a star moving away from Earth shifts toward the red end of the spectrum, while a star moving toward Earth shifts toward the blue end. When Hubble observed the light spectrum of several galaxies, he found a red shift, indicating that the galaxies were moving away from the Milky Way. He also noticed that galaxies located further away exhibited a greater shift toward red, which meant they were expanding outward more rapidly than proximate galaxies, and thus confirmed Lemaître's previous observations.

George Gamow, a Russian-born physicist working in the United States and a strong advocate of Lemaitre's primeval atom theory, suggested that the universe's supply of hydrogen and helium was created as a result of the extreme heat generated during the Big Bang. He proposed that the amount of hydrogen in the universe is three times the amount of helium, and tasked his cosmology student Ralph Alpher with developing these calculations as part of his doctoral dissertation. Gamow and Alpher published *The Origin of Chemical Elements* in April 1948, and it became known as the Alpher-Bethe-Gamow theory. Later that year, Alpher teamed up with physicist Robert Herman to conclude that the remaining heat from the Big Bang ought to be detectable as radiation, which later came to be known as the cosmic microwave background radiation (CMBR).

The discovery of the origin of hydrogen and helium was truly significant, but it also led scientists to question where the rest of the elements in our universe came from. In the 1950s, Fred Hoyle and his team of physicists—Geoffrey Burbidge, Margaret Burbidge, and William Alfred Fowler—began their investigation into how chemical elements were created. By observing the spectral lines that stars produced, and a variety of laboratory experiments, they concluded that chemical elements had been synthesized in the nuclear furnace of stars. When stars die and supernova, they release elements into the universe, which are later incorporated into the makeup of other stars and planets. In 1957, the scientists published their findings in the renowned paper B^2FH, named for the initials of the four scientists. Their profound insight aided our understanding of the origins of the physical elements, and left us to ponder the remarkable fact that every atom that makes up our body was once inside a star.

In 1964, at the Bell Labs in New Jersey, radio astronomers Arno Penzias and Robert Wilson used a large horn antenna to map audio signals generated in the Milky Way. However, as they listened, their audio systems encountered a strange static noise in the microwave range that seemed to be coming simultaneously from all directions. They initially assumed that the dish had malfunctioned, since pigeons had been nesting in it, but the noise continued after removing the birds and could not be attributed to any star, galaxy, or celestial object. As Penzias and Wilson tried to figure out what was wrong with their equipment, they learned that a group of Princeton University physicists were conducting ongoing experiments in search of low-level radiation left over from the Big Bang. Penzias and Wilson invited the physicists to examine their findings, and sure enough, the Princeton team realized the two radio astronomers had already found what they were looking for. The mysterious noise was the cosmic microwave background radiation caused by the colossal explosion that created our universe. For their exciting discovery, Penzias and Wilson received the Nobel Prize in Physics in 1978, and the Big Bang theory came to be the universally accepted model for the origin of our universe.

Since the 20th century, billions of dollars have been invested into developing highly sophisticated instruments to provide researchers with a clearer picture of our universe in order to better understand the laws that govern it. There are hundreds of terrestrial observatories across the globe, and more than a dozen space telescopes orbiting the planet, and these devices are capable of collecting data from all types of frequency ranges: infrared, ultraviolet, X-ray, gamma ray, microwave, radio, and visible light. Thousands of particle accelerators have been manufactured to investigate the bizarre reactions that occur on a microscopic scale when subatomic particles smash into one another. Supercomputers are able to run simulations of cosmic events such as supernovas, black holes, star and galaxy formations, and even the very moment the Big Bang brought the entire universe into existence. Occupying the space of an entire warehouse, a supercomputer can accomplish in one hour what a home computer would need 20 years to achieve. Due to these sophisticated technologies, researchers now understand how long the universe has been in existence, the quantity of matter it contains, how stars and planets are formed, and how the universe functions, so let us now turn our attention to the Big Bang phenomenon itself.

The Big Bang Theory

If we wish to comprehend the origin of our world on a fundamental level, we must attempt to understand the events of the Big Bang and the physical laws of science it revealed. The Big Bang represents the origin of space and time itself, and though we do not yet know how or why it occurred, we now possess the technology to observe and analyze its aftermath. The Big Bang theory describes the evolution of our cosmos according to the laws of physics, but it does not explain *why* the universe was created. The origin of this event remains the greatest scientific mystery of all time, and the more we learn about the universe, the closer we come to understanding its conception. Although this information may be rather complicated and difficult to comprehend, it is critical to present in order to illustrate just how much we have already discovered about the nature of our cosmos.

Everything we see in our present universe was previously enclosed in an infinitely dense, scorching singularity containing an unimaginable amount of energy. All laws of physics that we know today did not yet exist; they are responsible only for the structure of the universe resulting from the blast. For reasons not yet fully understood, this minute singularity exploded 13.8 billion years ago, and the universe came into being everywhere at once. Since space itself had been nonexistent prior to the explosion, every single point in space was created at the exact moment the Big Bang occurred.

Events unfolded so rapidly during the first moments of the explosion that scientists developed a new unit of time, known as Planck time, where one Plank time amounts to roughly 10^{-43} seconds. Immediately following the Big Bang, the universe was the size of a mere atom with a temperature of 10^{40} °K. The four forces of nature—gravity, strong nuclear, weak nuclear, and electromagnetic—existed in a singularity known as the superforce. At the end of this first Planck time, gravity split from the superforce as the universe expanded and cooled to a temperature of 10^{32} °K. The force of gravity would later be responsible for shaping the universe and forming the stars, planets, and galaxies within it.

At 10^{-36} seconds, the strong nuclear force split off from the superforce as the temperature of the universe cooled to 10^{27} °K. The strong nuclear force is responsible for stabilizing an atom by binding neutrons and protons in its nucleus, thus preventing the atom from disintegrating. As the nuclear force separated itself from the superforce, it triggered a phenomenon known as inflation, an event that points to the universe expanding instantaneously from the size of a proton to roughly the size of a grapefruit. This accelerated expansion of space, thought to have occurred between 10^{-36} and 10^{-32} seconds (faster than the speed of light), caused the volume of the universe to increase exponentially and uniformly in all directions, similar to the way a balloon inflates. When scientists measured the cosmic microwave background radiation (CMBR), their equipment registered identical readings in multiple locations, suggesting similar characteristics throughout the depths of space. They also found that galaxies were evenly dispersed, which pointed to a past cosmic event that had caused the compressed components to instantaneously spread out, stabilizing their temperatures and positions in the universe.

As the clock reached roughly 10^{-12} seconds and the temperature 10^{15} °K, the remaining two forces—the weak nuclear force and the electromagnetic force—separated. The weak nuclear force is responsible for radioactive decay, and is also the force behind the conversion of protons into neutrons and vice versa. By changing the charge of a quark inside the proton or the neutron in an atom, the weak nuclear force could alter the element itself. For example, a Carbon 14 atom with six protons and eight neutrons decays to a

Nitrogen 14 atom with seven protons and seven neutrons. The electromagnetic force is comprised of both the electricity and magnetism that we see and use in our daily lives. The electromagnetic force allows the charged particles to interact with each other, and binds electrons in their orbitals around the atom's nucleus.

While the universe expanded as heated energy, it simultaneously cooled, allowing this energy to transform into subatomic particles—the building blocks of matter. This process took place between 10^{-12} seconds and 10^{-6} seconds after the Big Bang, when the temperature of the universe had dropped to 10^{13} °K. As this pure energy produced matter, it also produced anti-matter, which could have eliminated everything in existence, since particles of anti-matter are much like particles of matter, but have a negative charge rather than a positive one. When these two types of particles collide, they eliminate one another with a nuclear explosion. An equal amount of matter and anti-matter will cancel one another out, and such an occurrence would have resulted in a completely vacant universe after the Big Bang. Fortunately, this event produced a billion and one particles of matter for every billion particles of anti-matter. Every single extra particle of matter that survived collisions with anti-matter is responsible for giving us the stars and galaxies we know today. The universe now contained quarks—the smallest substructures of an atom.

In 2000, scientists conducted a series of experiments to better understand how quarks came into existence and how these fundamental particles behaved during the creation of the universe. In order to observe how energy can be converted to atoms, researchers needed to reach a temperature of four trillion degrees Kelvin using the help of a particle accelerator. One of these magnificent feats of engineering is the Relativistic Heavy Ion Collider (RHIC) at the Brookhaven National Laboratories in Long Island, New York. This machine speeds up gold nuclei to nearly the speed of light in a 2.4-mile-wide (3.9 km) ring and slams them into each other at a rate of 78,000 times per second. These fantastic collisions have enough energy to not only tear the nuclei into protons and neutrons, but further reduce the protons and neutrons into quarks. After five years of experimentation and careful analysis, researchers understood that the quarks formed just after the Big Bang existed in a liquid state due to extremely high temperatures. This revolutionized our view of the cosmos: in its formative state, our universe consisted of nothing more than a soup-like material made up of quarks.

Another major event—the formation of the Higgs field—occurred between 10^{-12} seconds and 10^{-6} seconds, but well into the 20th century, scientists still could not yet comprehend how rudimentary particles of matter first exhibited mass. However, in 1964, British physicist Peter

Higgs suggested a mathematical model describing an invisible field which permeated the entire universe and was responsible for giving particles their mass. He theorized that this region consisted of particles which would later be known as Higgs bosons, which interact with elementary particles of matter as they pass through the field, thus giving the particles mass. The more often a particle interacts with the field, the greater its mass. As the mathematical calculations behind the theory appeared sound, scientists speculated that the Higgs boson could be detected in a powerful particle accelerator because the collision of subatomic particles would pinch Higgs bosons loose from the Higgs field, if it indeed existed.

This theory could not be tested until construction was completed on the most ambitious piece of scientific equipment to date. The Large Hadron Collider (LHC) in Switzerland required the collaborative efforts of 10,000 scientists and engineers from more than 100 countries during the 10 years it took to assemble. Approximately the size of a city, and with a price tag of 4.75 billion dollars, the LHC was designed to recreate the events that took place a millionth of a second after the Big Bang. The LHC consists of a concrete circular tunnel with a circumference of 17 miles (27 km) resting 574 feet (175 m) underground. This machine smashes protons or lead nuclei into each other at nearly the speed of light. For a tiny fraction of a second, the

23

charged energy it produces is enough to simulate the explosion of the Big Bang. Seven detectors capture these events with advanced cameras, the largest of which is five stories tall and weighs 7,000 tons. The LHC's data is collected on 170 supercomputer centers in 36 different countries, making it the largest collaborative network in the world. A group of 3,800 scientists spent five years hunting for the Higgs boson, and on July 4, 2012, confirmed its discovery. Peter Higgs had first developed his theory 50 years before it was verified by the most powerful and advanced piece of technology on the planet, and he received the Nobel Prize in Physics on December 10, 2013. The efforts of Higgs and his team offered researchers insight into the physical laws of our universe and how objects in space behaved when the universe was less than one second old.

As the universe further expanded and cooled, the strong nuclear force took hold of quarks and clumped them into groups of three, but the temperature remained too high for these particles to bond and form protons and neutrons. This took place between 10^{-6} seconds and one second after the Big Bang when the temperature dropped to 10^{10} °K and the universe had expanded to the size of our solar system. As the first second of the universe ticked by, the protons and neutrons that would later form the elemental atoms of our universe were created. All the physical laws governing our universe were established by this early moment in time, leaving us with an astonishing notion to contemplate—the one-second-old universe already contained everything we see today in our modern world.

At just one second old, the universe was 1,000 times the size of our solar system and consisted of a blistering plasma-like fluid of matter particulate and radiation. At this point, electrons and positrons which possess opposite charges, were colliding and annihilating one another. These collusions emitted energy in the form of photons—the elementary particles of light—though at this time, the universe remained too dense for light to escape.

Once the temperature of the universe had cooled to roughly 10^9 °K, protons and neutrons bonded together to produce the atoms of the first periodic element—hydrogen. In a period of less than 20 minutes, 25% of the hydrogen in the universe had fused into helium and trace amounts of lithium during Big Bang nucleosynthesis.

The universe continued to expand and cool at extremely rapid rates during the Matter-Dominated Period. During this era—which began roughly 47,000 years after the Big Bang—the universe was filled with particles of matter such as protons, electrons, and atomic nuclei. This matter constantly bombarded the photons, impairing their ability to travel freely through the opaque plasma that made up the universe. 370,000 years after the Big Bang, as the temperature dropped to 3,000 °K, electrons fell into orbit around the nuclei and formed neutral hydrogen and helium atoms. Since a greater volume of space now existed in the universe, the trapped photons bouncing around the electrons and protons could now travel freely through the universe as flashes of light. As this light escaped the plasma-like substance, the universe became increasingly transparent and slowly began to take the shape we recognize today.

To capture this past event, NASA launched the Cosmic Background Explorer Satellite (COBE) in 1989, which measured the temperature across space and offered researchers the first glimpses of our universe during its formation. These images provided a "picture" of the cosmic microwave background radiation (CMBR) as it appeared 370,000 years after the Big Bang, the approximate time during which light first escaped. In 2001, the United States launched an advanced satellite to obtain even more precise images of the CMBR with the Wilkinson Microwave Anisotropy Probe (WMAP). This satellite was positioned one million miles (1.6 million km) from Earth, so that no celestial bodies could restrict its view or affect its imaging during the five years that WMAP scanned the sky. In May 2009, the European Space Agency launched the Planck Satellite to orbit the sun and continuously record the temperature of the universe. This satellite was so accurate that it was capable of measuring the temperature of the CMBR to one-millionth of a degree.

The images that COBE, WMAP, and Planck satellites provided depicted the period approximately 370,000 years after the Big Bang, when the universe was trillions of miles wide and mainly consisted of hydrogen and helium clouds dissipating throughout space. It took 200 million years for these gases to create the first stars, which marked the earliest instances of light in our universe. The first galaxy formed between 300-500 million years after the Big Bang, as did countless others in the subsequent eight billion years. Five billion years ago, gravity took hold of gas and dust in a corner of our galaxy and created a star that turned out to be our sun. Soon after, Earth and other planets began to form from the leftover dust and gas in our solar system and orbit this star.

The current estimate of the number of stars in our universe is one septillion or 1×10^{24} stars. The comparison often used to illustrate this unimaginable number is that there are 10 times more stars in the universe than grains of sand in the world's desserts and beaches. We are extremely fortunate to have as many stars as we do, since without them, all matter in the universe (except for the hydrogen and helium produced by the Big Bang) would not exist. All elements on the periodic table following hydrogen and helium originated from a star, meaning that every atom that makes up your body was once formed inside the core of a star.

Additionally, scientists estimate that at least one planet orbits every star in our universe, giving us approximately the same number of planets as stars. Our Milky Way Galaxy has a diameter of 105,000 light years and zips through space at 1.3 million miles per hour (2 million km/hr). Our solar system orbits the center of the galaxy, 27,000 light years away on one of its outer arms, while spinning and whirling through space at 45,000 miles per hour (72,000 km/hr). Earth orbits the sun at 67,000 miles per hour (108,000 km/hr) while rotating on its axis at 1,000 miles per hour (1,600 km/hr).

As our universe had a beginning, it will also have an end. The Big Bang remains ongoing, and our universe continues to expand at an extremely rapid rate. Though we understand very little about dark energy—the force that accelerates the expansion of the universe and increases the distance between galaxies—scientists are able to observe its effects on other celestial bodies in space. If dark energy continues operating as it has previously, in approximately 17 billion years, the stars and galaxies will completely tear apart in an event named the Big Rip. Matter will cease to exist and the universe will become utterly void of light and life.

This represents our current prediction for the end of the universe, but since we do not yet fully comprehend dark energy, all current theories remain up for revision as we gain new insights into the workings of the universe. Any additional discoveries would augment the Big Bang theory, potentially modifying certain attributes of this model to provide us with a more accurate view of the universe.

Formation of Stars

Over the course of history, stars in the night sky have been the subject of awe and wonder, often playing a central role in the mythology of ancient cultures. The star closest to us, our sun, has been worshiped and deified by nearly all prehistoric civilizations as an integral part of our existence. However, over the ages, our views of the stars came to differ greatly once scientific investigation into these luminous bodies began to eradicate the mysticism behind them. The invention and continual improvement of the telescope and other advanced technologies allowed astronomers to record and evaluate their characteristics, and today we possess a solid understanding of the properties of stars, including how they are born, live, and will eventually die.

The ingredients for creating a star are hydrogen, gravity, and time, and since plenty of these components are readily available, it is no surprise to find our universe densely populated with them. Stars are shaped by interstellar clouds of dust and gas called nebulas which contain 99% gas and one percent dust. A star begins to form when a nebula collapses under the weight of its own gravity, and there are two main causes for this collapse: the direct collision of two such clouds, or the shockwave from a nearby exploding star slamming into a nebula.

When a nebula collapse commences, the force of gravity draws in the surrounding gas and dust to form a swirling vortex-like structure that becomes hotter as it condenses. Over the course of hundreds of thousands of years, this cloud increases in size until it forms a gigantic flat disc larger than our solar system. In the center of this disc, hydrogen gas is crushed into a dense fireball that reaches inferno-like temperatures. Pressure builds until jets of gas multiple light years wide explode from the center of the disc. During the next half-million years, its center becomes smaller, denser, and hotter until temperatures reach 15 million degrees Celsius, at which point hydrogen atoms undergo nuclear fusion. This explosion releases a massive amount of energy, and a star that will live for billions of years is officially born.

The creation process of stars remained a mystery until Albert Einstein formulated $E=MC^2$, demonstrating that matter possesses energetic potential locked within its atoms. This concept helped researchers comprehend exactly how stars sustained themselves while continuously releasing massive amounts of energy. A 20th century invention known as a tokamak, which recreates the process of nuclear fusion in a star, greatly enhanced our ability to understand the precise process of nuclear fusion.

Inside a tokamak, a magnetic container holds a blistering, concentrated plasma-like solution. Ordinarily, hydrogen atoms with the same charge repel each other, but when they are heated to 150 million degrees Celsius, the hydrogen atoms move at incredible speeds and cannot avoid smashing into one another. At this point, nuclear fusion occurs and these hydrogen atoms form helium, releasing a small amount of pure energy in the process. Helium weighs less than hydrogen, and the energy released during this process accounts for the mass lost between the two atoms. A tokamak can only perform this operation for a fraction of a second before fusion is lost, yet inside stars this process continues uninterrupted for billions of years. Because stars are so enormous, the force of gravity compresses this engine of heated fusion, giving stars the ability to shine while sustaining fusion at a rate of one billion nuclear bombs exploding per second. Once a star is born, a tug-of-war battle commences between the energy released from nuclear fusion and the force of gravity. Nuclear fusion attempts to blast the star apart; yet is unable to do so since gravity seeks to crush the star to its tiniest possible size. It is precisely this constant struggle between gravity and nuclear fusion that keeps the star in equilibrium and prevents it from exploding.

Death of Stars

The manner in which stars die depends on their size. When the hydrogen in a star the size of our sun runs out, fusion in the star's core slows, at which point gravity begins to crush the star. Fusion continues to heat the gas in the outer layers of the star, and this gas expands in a final effort to combat the crushing force of gravity before finally burning out.

Our sun, considered only a mid-sized star, burns 600 million tons of hydrogen in its core every second. Over the next five to seven billion years, this fuel source will deplete and our sun will begin to die, during which time it will expand to 256 times its current size and become a red giant. As thermonuclear fusion progresses, and as the sun converts the hydrogen in its core to helium, its outer layer will expand and produce a visible reddish hue. Temperatures on Earth will reach thousands of degrees, the oceans will evaporate, and the sun will incinerate our planet, along with Mercury and Venus. At this point, our sun will fuse helium into carbon, and an explosion from inside its core will strip away the sun's outer layers. The sun will slowly die, leaving behind its compressed core—a white dwarf roughly the size of the Earth, yet one million times denser. Fusion will have concluded by this point, and scientists theorize that inside the white dwarf's core will be a massive crystallized carbon rock—a diamond—thousands of miles wide. This white dwarf will contain enough carbon and oxygen to shine for billions of years before ultimately becoming a black dwarf once it runs out of fuel.

Type 1A and 2A Supernovas

The majority of stars in the universe orbit in pairs, and when one of the two stars dies and becomes a white dwarf, it begins drawing hydrogen and helium from its companion star. Slowly but surely, the white dwarf becomes heavier and denser as it enters an unstable state. In its core, oxygen and carbon begin fusing into iron. Iron absorbs energy which causes the core of the star to collapse onto itself and explode. This type of supernova is the source of nearly all iron in the universe. These explosions are known as Type 1A supernovas, and occur when the size of the star reaches exactly 1.4 times the size of the sun. At this stage, the star releases a consistent amount of light, making it and others like it an excellent source for measuring and comparing distances throughout the universe.

In contrast to smaller ones, large stars evolve in a short period of time, burn bright, and die out in one of the most spectacular ways possible—a type 2A supernova. The death of these giant stars creates the building blocks of our universe. When a star runs out of hydrogen, it begins fusing helium in its core and manufacturing heavier elements, which ultimately leads to the death of the star.

As a bombardment of helium atoms increases the temperature in the core of the star, helium converts to carbon, and later to oxygen. This process of fusion continues producing different elements according to their number on the periodic table, until the star creates iron, atomic number 26. Iron absorbs energy, and thus when a massive star begins to create this element, it is mere seconds before the star self-destructs. Once iron absorbs the energy created through fusion, fusion begins to lose its battle with gravity. When the iron core of the star collapses onto itself at a rate of one-fourth the speed of light, energy builds in the star's core until it supernovas. During the explosion, the elements that formed in the star's core during this process erupt into outer space.

As the blast tears through the star's outer layers, it creates elements heavier than iron, and continues down the periodic table: iron becomes cobalt, cobalt becomes nickel, then silver, gold, platinum, and finally, uranium. These heavier elements that did not exist within the star are formed by the heat of the explosion, and since these elements are formed in a brief instant, they are the rarest in the universe and hold the greatest value here on Earth. To put this dizzying concept into perspective, a type 2A supernova creates more energy in an instant than our sun will create during its entire lifespan.

When a star approximately eight times the size of our sun undergoes a type 2A supernova, it leaves behind a neutron star. The core of the star—condensed from the size of a planet to the size of a city—spins at a rate of up to 700 times per second. Some spin so fast that they cause beams of light to pulse out of the north and south poles of the star, which is known as a pulsar. When stars up to 30 times larger than our sun explode, they leave behind a neutron star called a magnetar—a neutron star possessing a magnetic field. When stars more than 100 times the size of our sun explode, they go into hypernovas that release gamma ray radiation, the deadliest and most powerful type of radiation. Because of the star's massive size, gravity crushes its core into a black hole. The gamma ray radiation bursts from a black hole possess 100 million times more power than an ordinary supernova, and produce the brightest light in the universe.

This is the story of these innumerous, incredible bodies that light up our universe. Without their birth, life, and fantastic death, the universe would be dark, empty, and void of life—all known matter would not exist. Our sun, planets, and all life (including ourselves) are comprised of elements that once burst from stars. An estimated 275 million stars undergo the process of birth and death every day in our universe—that's 3,183 stars per second. I hope that the next time you look up and enjoy the beauty of the stars in our night sky, you can truly appreciate the connection we have with them, for we are nothing but star dust.

Planet Earth

Home to millions of creatures, our planet is truly a remarkable example of the diversity of life. Only when we see the Earth from outer space do we develop a deeper appreciation of its enormity and gain a surreal sense of our own insignificance. Everything we value exists upon this blue marble floating through space, but how did the Earth form? As we shall see, the cosmic events that gave birth to our solar system and our planet reveal an extraordinary history.

As previously discussed, stars form when a nebula collapses after colliding with another, or from the shockwave of a supernova slamming into a nebula. Scientists believe the latter formed our solar system, causing a giant molecular cloud of hydrogen and helium to collapse. Other massive supernovae expelled the heavier elements such as carbon, nitrogen, oxygen, iron, and silicon that were essential to life on Earth.

Approximately five billion years ago, the shockwave of a neighboring supernova slammed into a nebula, implanting it with additional heavy elements. This shockwave caused the nebula to collapse and begin rotating, thus initiating the creation of our solar system, as well as many neighboring star systems. A small pocket inside this cloud—the solar nebula—buckled and began to spin. As its rotation rapidly accelerated, gravity heated and compressed matter within the solar nebula until it flattened into what astronomers call a proto-planetary disc. After 100,000 years, this disc-shaped nebula had almost completely collapsed. Because of the immense pressure building in the center of the solar nebula, a ball of hydrogen and helium—a proto-star—began to glow. As this proto-star became hotter and denser, its immense gravitational pull devoured nearly all the gas and dust that made up the solar nebula. Eventually, 99.99% of all the gas and dust in the solar nebula was drawn to its center, while the remaining 0.01% of the mass spinning on the outskirts later formed the planets, asteroids, comets, and meteorites of our solar system. Fifty million years after the collapse commenced, temperatures in the core of the proto-star reached the critical threshold where hydrogen fuses into helium, and our sun ignited. At the time of its formation, the sun possessed enough energy to shine for the next 10-12 billion years.

The birth of the sun was not the only significant cosmic event taking place during this period—gravity acting on minute particles of matter set in motion the extensive process of forming the eight planets in our solar system. The particles of dust orbiting the nebula's center began to gently collide and adhere to one another due to the electrostatic forces of nature.

Once these balls of dust formed, they began their transformation into rocks. As lightning spread throughout the activated nebula and struck the balls of dust, they reach temperatures of 1,650 °C. It took only a few minutes for the dust balls to cool and harden into rocks, yet they were now on their way to becoming colossal planets. When these rocks reached the size of asteroids, the force of gravity intensified and continued drawing additional material toward their center, including smaller asteroids.

As this clump of asteroids gradually grew to hundreds of miles wide, its internal gravity began to change the shape of its structure. As mass increases, so does gravitational force, which eventually crushes the rocks into smaller fragments. These rocks naturally became round over time, and after this continued for millions of years, our solar system consisted of a dozen or so proto-planets. This violent process repeated itself for the next 100 million years, and the proto-planets combined into the eight full-size planets we know today. The remaining material that did not coalesce into planets formed the asteroid belt between Mars and Jupiter, the Kuiper Belt beyond the orbit of Neptune, and the

Oort Cloud, a collection of billions of comets nearly one light year from the sun.

Due to this constant asteroid bombardment, the Earth consisted of molten rock and metal, and in this liquefied state, the heavier iron and nickel were drawn to the center of the developing planet, while the molten rock drifted toward the edge, eventually cooling and forming the planet's crust. This was one of the most critical stages in our planet's formation—as the molten iron spun and swirled, it created the Earth's magnetic field, shielding the planet from outer space's lethal radiation.

Approximately 4.5 billion years ago, a proto-planet the size of Mars named Theia slammed into the Earth. Fortunately, the two celestial bodies did not directly collide, because such a collision would have annihilated our planet. Instead, the force of this impact destroyed Theia and returned our planet to a molten state. The collision also rocketed billions of tons of the Earth's crust into outer space, which eventually clumped into two rocky bodies orbiting the Earth. Over time, gravity brought these two bodies close enough to collide and coalesce into the moon. In 1969, the Apollo Lunar Module landed on the moon, enabling astronauts to gather and return to earth with 840 pounds (381 kg) of moon rocks. Scientists determined their chemical composition was identical to that of the Earth's outer layers, thus confirming that Theia's collision with Earth broke off a portion of its crust, which later became the moon.

What happened next remains critical as to why Earth would eventually possess the capacity to harbor life. During its formation, the sun had vaporized all water present in the inner solar system, so the only water in existence remained locked in the ice collected on asteroids and comets of the Kuiper and asteroid belts. The larger planets—Jupiter, Saturn, Neptune, and Uranus—did not maintain consistent orbits. Each time Saturn orbited the sun, Jupiter orbited it twice, and when these two planets aligned, an event known as orbital resonance took place, and the force of gravity pulled Jupiter and Saturn along a parallel course. The resonance of Saturn and Jupiter destabilized not only these two giants, but countless other celestial bodies, including Neptune and Uranus. This occurrence also scattered the water-filled asteroids and comets of the asteroid and Kuiper belts across our solar system, placing them on a collision course with the developing planets.

The age known as the Late Heavy Bombardment Period took place between 3.9 and 3.8 billion years ago and lasted between 20-200 million years. Many of these icy asteroids hit our planet from all directions—not one foot of Earth was spared, and remnants of this cataclysmic bombardment can be seen in the thousands of craters on the moon. As the Earth continued to cool, its crust and mantel reformed into the planetary shape we recognize today, with an abundance of water on its surface.

At this time, the moon was 10 times closer to the Earth than it is today, exhibiting a greater gravitational pull, causing the tides to slow the Earth's rotation. This process, known as tidal friction, occurs when the ocean tides push against the land, causing enough friction to slow the Earth's rotation. The moon's orbit around the Earth also maintained the Earth's rotation at a constant angle, which served to stabilize the climate on our planet.

It is important to contemplate and appreciate the fact that Earth exists simply because every single fantastic event, from the moment the universe came into existence to the formation of our planet, took place under perfectly precise conditions. For Earth-like planets to harbor life, they require water, a stabilizing moon, a protective magnetic field, and a favorable location relative to its sun. This means that due to its enormous size, the universe could be full of Earth-like planets. Although these conditions are difficult to come by, at least 100 billion planets exist in our galaxy, not to mention the 100 billion other galaxies in the observable universe, so some other form of life—however primitive—must exist somewhere, and we are most likely to find it on a planet that is hospitable to water.

Until the discovery of the first exoplanet in 1992, it was unsure where—if at all—planets outside our solar system existed, but as of December 2020, 4,379 exoplanets have been observed. Scientists discovered these exoplanets using one of two methods: by looking for a star to wobble from the gravitational push and pull of the planets orbiting it, or by observing the diminishing light of a star as a planet passes in front of it.

Depending on a planet's speed, scientists are able to calculate its distance from the star it orbits, and can easily determine if it is located in the Goldilocks Zone. In our solar system, this area contains Earth and Mars, and generally refers to an area of space that is an ideal distance from the star it orbits, where the temperature is neither too hot nor too cold, but just right. By examining these specific areas around other stars, we can focus our search for extra-terrestrial life on the planets likely to contain water.

We still do not fully comprehend our universe, but our extensive wealth of knowledge testifies to the reliability of the scientific method as well as the brilliance and determination of the technical mind. The ingenuity and passion of early scientific pioneers has granted all of us the opportunity to comprehend our place, and more importantly, our role in the universe.

Astrophysicist Neil deGrasse Tyson states that the laws of nature are unbreakable—they do not vary from culture to culture or time to time and they hold true throughout the cosmos. If you do not wish to accept this reality, you will need to defend your view against Nobel Prize winners, astronauts who have travelled to space, advanced technology and machinery such as the Large Hadron Collider, and finally, the scientific disciplines of mathematics and physics.

The chain of events that set off the moment our universe came into existence are truly extraordinary. Becoming aware of the connection you have with the universe will allow you to realize that you are a part of it and you are here because of it. It took a number of scientific prodigies working over hundreds of years to gain the scientific knowledge we possess today—it may be quite difficult to comprehend, but this does not mean it can be ignored, or that if you have been unaware of it, that the information does not hold true. You can learn about it little by little every day, open up your mind, and begin to understand *who* and *where* you are in the universe.

CHAPTER TWO

THE JOURNEY OF LIFE ON EARTH

The Journey of Life on Earth

There are two main schools of thought concerning the origin of life on Earth: panspermia and abiogenesis. Panspermia hypothesizes that frozen organisms came to Earth embedded in meteoroids or asteroids, which would have taken place during the early stages of Earth's formation, at the time when it exhibited a great deal of activity from cosmic collisions. Panspermia proposes that dormant bacteria originating from other planets hitched a ride on a rocky celestial body that eventually collided with the Earth. Once Earth's conditions were suitable to sustain life, the bacteria activated, spread, and eventually evolved.

Abiogenesis, on the other hand, points to life originating on Earth from inorganic matter through a series of chemical reactions in pools of primordial soup containing amino acids, the building blocks of organic matter. Molecules of these compounds would have continuously collided with one another for millions of years, until just the correct sequence happened to occur and the chain reaction of life began. Due to the fact that Earth lacked an oxygen-rich atmosphere to shield it from the sun's damaging radiation, the majority of evidence points to abiogenesis taking place at the bottom of the ocean. On Earth's surface, this radiation would have broken down the amino acid sequences as soon as they had formed. On the sea floor, water seeped into the Earth through cracks in the crust, collecting gases and

45

minerals as its temperature increased. This searing chemical mixture spewed back to the surface through hydrothermal vents in the sea floor, and from this primordial soup, life is believed to have originated approximately 3.8 billion years ago. These chemicals formed the correct sequence to create microscopic single-celled organisms that eventually evolved into prokaryotes. These microorganisms were able to replicate at a higher rate than they could be destroyed, and so began the earliest forms of life on Earth.

A Brief Overview of Biological Evolution

The theory of evolution is the natural mechanism that explains how life on our planet diversified. The variety of incredible organisms in the world today, as well as evidence of fossil records demonstrate how certain organisms have adapted and changed over time. Biological evolution can be defined as any change in the heritable traits within a population across multiple generations, a process which may also result in the creation of an entirely new species.

When the DNA of an organism is replicated, random copying errors occasionally occur. Known as mutations, these irregularities alter an organism's DNA that will affect its offspring immediately or several generations later. Change brought about by a mutation has the potential to be beneficial, harmful, or neutral. If the change is harmful, it is unlikely that the offspring will survive to reproduce, so the mutation will ultimately die out and be eliminated from the genetic code. If the change appears to provide benefits, the offspring are likely to be more successful than other members of their species, and will therefore reproduce more frequently. The process of eliminating the less desirable mutations and passing on more desirable ones is called natural selection, a theory credited to Charles Darwin in the mid-1800s. As mutations occurred over long periods of time, this process eventually formed new species. Over the course of millions of years, the processes of mutation and natural selection have created and fine-tuned the features of all the unique organisms that we see in the fossil record and in the world today.

Every species is subject to natural selection, which is driven by environmental influences such as predators, parasites, toxins, habitat or climate changes, and competition within species. Each individual inherits a unique set of characteristics from their parents that either help or hinder their survival. Members of the species with unfavorable traits tend to have less reproductive success, while those with desirable traits pass on their enhanced features in order for the next generation to better survive in a particular environment, thus having a better chance to reproduce.

To illustrate this process, let us take a look at Darwin's finches on the Galapagos Islands of Ecuador. Approximately two million years ago, a small group of finches was blown onto the Galapagos Islands, most likely due to a large storm. The birds found themselves in a new environment with an abundance of food and a lack of predators. They reproduced rapidly, and the islands were soon teeming with these birds, but once food sources became scarce, the finches began to compete for survival, and the process of natural selection began.

Since each finch possessed a unique set of traits, some birds found themselves more adaptable to certain environments than other members of their species. The beaks of some were better suited for digging up worms, while the beaks of others were more efficient at cracking seeds open. Therefore, these finches began to occupy different ecological niches where they experienced less competition from other members of their species. Over many generations, the beneficial beak traits became increasingly specialized, enabling the finches to be more successful in their respective environmental niches. Eventually, the finches in each habitat diverged so greatly that they were no longer able to mate, making them two completely different species. Today, there are 14 diverse finch species living on the Galapagos Islands, all descendants of the small group that originally arrived two million years ago. We have seen from these birds how the process of evolution can create new species over a span of time, so let us now return to early microscopic life forms entering their first stages of development.

As life took shape on our planet, it began to populate the oceans, and the process of biological evolution ran its course, resulting in many diverse species of prokaryotes. Prokaryotes are cells with no nucleus or other membrane-bound organelles, and their genetic material floats inside the cell. On the other hand, eukaryotic cells store DNA inside the nucleus and possess multiple organelles that carry out important functions for the cell. Prokaryotes would later evolve into eukaryotes—the cells from which all plants, animals, and human beings originated.

Approximately 3.5 billion years ago, a new form of bacteria evolved in shallow oceans that would change the course of life on our planet. This organism, called cyanobacteria, is the main reason that all life forms, including human beings, exist on land today. Cyanobacteria developed a process known as photosynthesis to convert sunlight into nutrients by transforming carbon dioxide and water into glucose, a simple form of sugar. This chemical reaction releases oxygen as a waste byproduct, and these bacteria colonies reproduced at astounding speeds, since water and sunlight are their only requirements for survival and reproduction. Cyanobacteria oxygenated the ocean, causing minute traces of iron in the water to rust. These particles fell to the ocean floor, where they eventually formed an iron-rich bedrock. Most of Earth's iron exists within its molten core, so we can thank cyanobacteria for the abundance of iron on the planet's surface, as well as the oxygen we breathe today, since all plants evolved from variations of cyanobacteria.

During this period, Earth lacked an atmosphere to protect it from the sun's harmful radiation. As the oxygen produced by cyanobacteria saturated the iron in the oceans, it began escaping the water and moving into the atmosphere. Previously, the oxygen had been bound to iron particles, but as time passed, the cyanobacteria produced more oxygen than the ocean's iron could contain. This natural phenomenon would eventually instigate the Great Oxidation Event, in which the air became so oxygen-rich that it poisoned nearly all prokaryotic species. In the upper atmosphere, the influx of oxygen reacted with the ultra-violet radiation of the sun, and created a surplus of ozone (O_3). Even though it occurred on a microscopic level, this was the greatest extinction in the Earth's history. Over time, the protective ozone layer built up and blocked the damaging ultra-violet rays of the sun, allowing the cells that survived the extinction to further develop.

Eukaryotic cells began their evolution between 2.1 and 1.6 billion years ago, and all plants and animals on our planet are made from these cells. Eukaryotes evolved due to the process of endosymbiosis, whereby one prokaryotic cell consumes another without digesting it. This process proved beneficial to both the host and the prey, and this single-celled organism eventually procured organelles, which helped the cell survive and reproduce, allowing for more complex life forms. Gradually, a number of eukaryotes began to collaborate with one another in a process known as symbiosis, wherein one cell carries out a specific task in exchange for a different cell carrying out another job, allowing both to survive as partners. Over time, these cells became so dependent on each other that one could not survive independently and as such, eukaryotic multicellular life arose. The first multicellular eukaryotic organisms were algae, as evidenced in the fossil record dating between 1.7 and 1.5 billion years ago. Life on Earth continued in this manner for another billion years, until more complex multicellular life forms emerged as a result of a major catastrophe.

Snowball Earth

Scientists contend that there have been at least two Snowball Earth glaciations, which occurred 710 and 640 million years ago. The most recent of these events proved significant for the evolution of life on Earth when a global ice age gripped our planet for ten million years. At this point in time, only one giant supercontinent existed near the equator. Because of this region's high heat and humidity, a process known as weathering occurred, whereby carbon dioxide combined with water vapor to form acid rain, which reacted with minerals imbedded in rocks on the Earth's surface, forming and trapping new carbon chemicals in the water. This mixture made its way into the oceans where the buildup of deposits eventually formed solid limestone on the sea floor. The carbon dioxide that once trapped heat in the Earth's atmosphere was now locked in limestone at the bottom of the sea. Because the acid rainfall removed an enormous amount of carbon dioxide from the atmosphere, the planet began to cool, and the volume of sea ice dramatically increased.

This triggered an additional cooling reaction due to the albedo effect, or the reflective capability of ice. Reflecting up to 80% of sunlight that strikes its surface, sea ice has one of the highest albedos and is the most natural sunlight reflector on the planet. By contrast, the oceans have the lowest albedo (less than 10%) on the planet, and absorb the majority of sunlight that reaches the water's surface, allowing the planet to retain heat.

During the Snowball Earth period, there was a great expanse of ice reflecting sunlight and heat back into the atmosphere, leaving a smaller volume of ocean to absorb and retain heat from the sun. During this global cooling event, the more ice that formed, the more heat was reflected back into the atmosphere instead of heating the Earth. The situation eventually reached a tipping point where ice approximately 0.6-mile-thick (1 km) covered the entire planet in an ice age that lasted ten million years. Ultimately, geological activities such as geysers and volcanos broke through the ice, ejecting greenhouse gases into the atmosphere. It took thousands of volcanoes releasing billions of tons of carbon dioxide over millions of years to trap the sunlight, increase the temperature of the Earth, and melt the ice.

The organisms that survived this freeze and adapted under the ice took the greatest leap in the evolution of life up to this point, as they evolved into the first complex creatures on Earth. Oxygen levels were a critical component of chemical and biological conditions required for complex forms of life to develop. Prior to this ice age, oxygen made up only one percent of the atmosphere, but increased to 21% afterwards. Scientists speculate this oxygen increase was due to a reaction between the ultraviolet rays of the sun and frozen water molecules, which produced and trapped hydrogen peroxide (H_2O_2) in the ice. As the ice melted, the hydrogen peroxide broke down, releasing oxygen into the oceans and atmosphere. Fossil records show that this surge in oxygen levels fueled the evolution of life from single to multi-cellular organisms. The cells inside these organisms continued to specialize in performing different bodily functions, which eventually led to the creation of organs. Around 600 million years ago, the beginnings of more complex slug-like creatures evolved with distinct features such as a head, stomach, and back.

The Cambrian Explosion

Roughly 541 million years ago, in a warm, oxygen-rich ocean, the Cambrian Explosion began. During this period of 13-25 million years, life produced tens of thousands of new animal and plant species. A combination of factors needed to be perfected in order to trigger this explosion of biodiversity, and the chemistry of the ocean underwent numerous changes, beginning with the high concentrations of oxygen caused by Snowball Earth. During this period, ocean levels continually fluctuated, and at their pinnacle, flooded low-lying parts of the landscape to create shallow seas rich in nutrients. Increased erosion dragged mineral-rich deposits of carbonates and phosphates back into the seas, which helped tiny organisms build shells and nuclei. As substrate mixed with ocean water, it led to the emergence of plankton, a crucial element in the food chain. The surge in nutrients increased the volume of food resources and habitable environments, allowing new organisms to thrive.

Due to these factors, we see more the familiar components of the struggle for survival, as well as predators and prey in direct conflict. Competition among new creatures further accelerated the evolutionary process and established the path on which life would progress over the next 500 million years. As such, many complex organisms evolved during the Cambrian Period and became the ancestors of all animal groups in existence today, including mollusks, arthropods, mammals, and humans. The most famous fossilized animals from the Cambrian Explosion are the trilobites: Pikaia, Wiwaxia, a five-eyed creature named Opabinia, and a top predator of the time, Anomalocaris.

The trilobites were arthropods; the ancestors of lobsters, scorpions, spiders, crustaceans, and insects. The trilobites are among the most successful and enduring of all prehistoric animals, diversifying into more than 17,000 species. Pikaia, the oldest known ancestor of modern vertebrates, was the first organism to have a head-like structure and a spinal cord. Wiwaxia was a small armored slug, and the five-eyed, predatory Opabinia captured its prey using a flexible claw arm attached to its head. Anomalocaris was a deadly giant shrimp-like creature up to three feet (0.9 m) in size with large eyes, razor-sharp teeth, and menacing limbs.

The Cambrian Period derives its name from the rocky outcrops of Cambria, California, where geologists

Adam Sedgwick and Roderick Murchison first discovered these types of animal fossils in the 1830s. In 1909, paleontologist Charles Walcott discovered well-preserved Cambrian fossils in the Burgess Shale of British Columbia, Canada, where he collected more than 60,000 fossils over the course of 15 years. The most famous discoveries came from the Chengjiang fossil bed in China, where in 1999, scientists began uncovering the extremely well-preserved fossils of Cambrian animals. The site contained at least 185 species of marine animals with both hard and soft tissues.

The Cambrian Explosion represented a fundamental revolution in biology, without which complex life would not have come to exist. Every complex macroscopic organism, including *Homo sapiens*, owes its existence to the events which unfolded during the 13-25 million years of the Cambrian Period. We ought to take a bit of time to appreciate the incredible changes that occurred during the Cambrian Explosion, for it is truly wondrous to pause and reflect on how profoundly this evolutionary revolution altered the course of life on Earth.

The First Great Mass Extinction Event

The Ordovician-Silurian mass extinction occurred roughly 444 million years ago, yet the reasons behind it are still under investigation. During this period, the Earth's crust consisted of three oceans and four supercontinents. The land remained void of life, but the oceans were full of corals, fish, and a multitude of other sea creatures. A later cataclysm would wipe out 85% of life in the seas, and although the cause of this extinction remains uncertain, scientists have proposed several potential scenarios.

The first hypothesis suggests that the movement of plate tectonics in the warm southern supercontinent, Gondwana, located in the South Polar Region, triggered another ice age. A second hypothesis looks to the supernova of a massive star within 6,000 light years of Earth, which would have emitted a gamma-ray burst of energy directly toward our planet. This destructive radiation torrent would have lasted only 10 seconds, but would have vaporized one-third of our ozone layer, leaving the creatures on Earth vulnerable to lethal doses of ultra-violet radiation from the sun. In addition to the deterioration of the ozone layer, the gamma-ray burst would have disassembled nitrogen and oxygen molecules in the atmosphere, producing a gaseous smog of nitrogen dioxide, which would have prevented sunlight from reaching Earth, and resulted in extreme global cooling. Though neither hypothesis can be substantiated, it is certain that a severe ice age wiped out 85% of life on Earth. The surviving species were able to cope with these new conditions, fill the ecological niches left by the extinction event, and take life on Earth in a whole new evolutionary direction.

The Migration of Life onto Land

Between 450 and 435 million years ago, the first plants begin to appear on land. During this time, the ozone layer had become thick enough to block the majority of the deadly radiation from the sun, allowing primitive life forms to survive outside the water. The first land plants are believed to have evolved from green algae living on the edge of shallow seas or lakes, and as plants made their move to land, arthropods such as millipedes and insects also began to appear on dry ground. In the next tens of millions of years, the land plants multiplied, pumping more and more oxygen into the atmosphere, which allowed it to block more of the lethal ultra-violet radiation from the sun. Now that the land was protected by a thicker ozone layer, nutrient-rich soil produced an abundance of food sources, and more complex animal life began to flourish.

The oldest known land-dwelling creature is a species of millipede named *Pneumodesmus newmani*. The first fossil of this creature, which is thought to be 428 million years old, was discovered in Scotland in 2004, and openings on its body that were used for gas exchange make it the first oxygen-breathing animal on land discovered to date. The oldest known fossilized insect—*Rhyniognatha hirsti*—dates back to between 407 and 396 million years ago.

The Second Great Mass Extinction Event

Though the exact length of the Late Devonian extinction remains uncertain, estimates range from 500,000 to 25 million years. A variety of reasons have been proposed for this mass extinction event that took place roughly 376 million years ago, including an asteroid impact, shifting plate tectonics, and the eruption of a super volcano. However, the Devonian Plant Hypothesis suggests that because plants were so abundant on land (and had been for more than 60 million years), their absorption of massive amounts of carbon dioxide from the atmosphere resulted in a global cooling event.

No matter which catastrophe or combination thereof caused this extinction, the planet experienced a global temperature drop, a major increase in glacier formation, and a significant reduction of sea levels. Ocean anoxia (oxygen shortages) made this extinction event particularly severe for marine organisms. By the end of the Late Devonian extinction, more than 70% of all species on the planet had become nonexistent, forcing the remaining life forms to adapt and evolve.

Approximately 375 million years ago, vertebrates begin their exodus from water to land, possibly due to ocean anoxia. One of the first vertebrates to make this transition was a fish-like creature known as *Tiktaalik*. The first fossilized remains of this ancient creature were unearthed in the Canadian Arctic in 2004. The neck of *Tiktaalik* allowed the organism to raise itself up, and fins utilized as legs permitted *Tiktaalik* to drag itself onto land. These fins had the beginnings of the bone structure shared by all vertebrates that walk on land today. *Tiktaalik* possessed a primitive version of an upper arm, forearm, and parts of a wrist, as well as gills, scales, lungs, and a crocodile-like head. This transitional species between fish and tetrapods is the ancestor of all four-legged vertebrates including amphibians, reptiles, dinosaurs, birds, and mammals. *Tiktaalik* only spent a short amount of time out of the water, but over a period of 15 million years, it developed stronger limbs and adapted to land, which allowed *Tiktaalik* to make the land its permanent home roughly 360 million years ago. Around the same time, terrestrial amphibians evolved from creatures like *Tiktaalik* to live fully terrestrial lives.

Between 320 and 310 million years ago, the first reptiles began to evolve from amphibians and populate the land. One of the first to do so was a small lizard-like creature 8-12 inches (20-30 cm) in length called *Hylonomus,* which possessed a new evolutionary adaptation—it could lay its eggs outside the water, something that no other organism had been capable of until this point. Because the hard eggshells contained plenty of water and nutrients for the developing offspring, these animals could now permanently leave the water to begin life on land.

Roughly 300 million years ago, the Earth began to take the shape we recognize today. The seas were brimming with fish, while insects, amphibians, and reptiles roamed the land, and atmospheric oxygen levels soared to 32% due to rich vegetation (it is 21% today). Due to these high levels of oxygen, the respiratory systems of insects became more efficient, allowing them to evolve into giants compared to their modern descendants. These creatures were monstrous: millipedes (*Arthropleura*) reached 7 feet (2 m) in length, scorpions (*Pulmonoscorpius*) were the size of wolves, and dragonflies (*Meganeura*) boasted a wingspan of more than two feet (70 cm) in length. As oxygen levels dropped and stabilized, these enormous insects could no longer adapt to their environment, and eventually became extinct.

Coal, Oil, and Natural Gas

All the coal, oil, and natural gas that powers our modern society is derived from plants and animals that died hundreds of millions of years ago, hence the term 'fossil fuels.' The majority of this energy source was deposited in the Carboniferous Period, which occurred between 360-300 million years ago and derives its name from carbon being the dominant element present in fossil fuels. During this period, swamps, trees, and plants blanketed the land, and the oceans were rich with algae. As vegetation and marine organisms died, they sank to the bottom of swamps and oceans, forming an organic layer called peat. Over thousands of years, the peat became covered with sand, clay, mud, and other minerals, eventually forming sedimentary rock. As more rocks formed, the pressure of this weight began to squeeze out water. Over millions of years, heat from the Earth and the pressure of overlying rocks transformed this mixture into coal. Similarly, oil (petroleum) and natural gas formed from dead plants and microscopic sea creatures, depending on how liquid or gaseous their mixture of the dead organic matter was.

With the arrival of the Permian period 298-252 million years ago, land on Earth had coalesced into one supercontinent called Pangaea, which was surrounded by a global ocean named Panthalassa. In the middle of Pangaea lay the largest desert the world had ever seen, which offered little in the way of plant life or other sources of food. Insects, reptiles, and amphibians also inhabited the land, but because they were better-suited to dry conditions, reptiles rose to dominance during this period.

The Third Great Mass Extinction Event

The End-Permian mass extinction, also known as the Great Dying, occurred roughly 252 million years ago, and wiped out 95% of all animal and plant species on Earth. It is the only mass extinction on record to have affected insects, and by the end of this period, 70% of terrestrial vertebrates and 96% of all marine species had become extinct.

Geologists and paleontologists learned of this mass extinction through sedimentary rocks deposits, in which each layer represented a period of time, with the most recent on top, and at the height of the Permian fossil record, we see a dramatic change. A green-blue-gray layer teaming with fossils points to a wet, lush period underneath a red layer void of fossils, which by contrast, indicates extremely dry conditions. From this geological confirmation, scientists observed that the global temperature of Earth rose 10 ℃ over a period of 100,000 years.

This vital clue indicated that the extinction had not been caused by an asteroid impact, because this would have resulted in a much quicker annihilation. This extinction is thought to have been caused by a destructive lava flow known as a flood basalt, and during the 1990s, evidence for such an occurrence was found in the Siberian Traps of Russia—a massive collection of volcanic rocks the size of Alaska. A flood basalt occurs when a large stretch of land breaks open, allowing vast amounts of lava to spew out of the Earth. After surveying this location, scientists concluded that the magma spew from the flood basalt of the Siberian traps covered an area the size of the United States in a 0.6-mile-thick (1 km) layer of molten rock. They also estimated that the Siberian traps erupted over a period of one million years, and produced nearly 3 million square miles (7.7 million square km) of lava.

By this point, 10% of the world's species had been eliminated. Fossil records indicate that plants were the first to be affected by the sulfur dioxide and carbon dioxide in the air. The eruptions released billions of tons of CO_2, saturating the atmosphere with 20 times more carbon dioxide than is present in our atmosphere today. The increase of CO_2 caused a 5 °C rise of Earth's temperature, and fossilized plants show evidence of this occurrence. Plants possess specialized holes

After years of research, scientists presented a succession of events that they believed led to the End-Permian mass extinction, which began when the Siberian traps released a tremendous amount of toxic lava, ash, and gases. The lava destroyed everything it touched and the ash blocked out the sun's rays, but the gases proved to be the most dangerous of all. Sulfur dioxide began to mix with the moisture in the atmosphere, turning into sulfuric acid, which fell to Earth as acid rain. The sulfuric acid that remained in the atmosphere reflected the sun's rays and cooled the planet.

called stomata to absorb CO_2 during photosynthesis, and the more carbon dioxide that is present in the air, the fewer stomata a plant needs to absorb it. Researchers observed a dramatic drop in the numbers of CO_2-absorbing stomata in fossilized plants of the End-Permian period, pointing to a massive spike in the amount of CO_2 in the atmosphere. As temperatures rose, areas near the equator stopped producing rain, leading to desertification of the landscape. Plants, as well as the herbivores and carnivores that depended upon them, began to perish in great numbers.

By this time, 35% of all species on the planet had been wiped out, and the oceans would soon experience a similar devastation. Within the Permian rocks, marine geologists and biologists found layers of black sediment lined with yeast, or fool's gold, indicating that the Permian oceans had been depleted of oxygen. As the oceans heated due to global warming, they failed to circulate oxygen and became stagnate. This lack of oxygen caused purple sulfur bacteria to thrive on the bottom of the oceans, producing hydrogen sulfide. As this poisonous gas rose from the bottom of the oceans, it killed everything it passed on its way to the surface. Fifty thousand years into the eruption of the Siberian Traps, 70% of all life on Earth had been destroyed.

As time went on, global temperatures shot up an additional 5 °C, killing another 25% of the creatures living on

Earth. This second deadly wave of rising temperatures was due to methane released from stores of frozen methane hydrate at the bottom of the oceans. This potent greenhouse gas warms the atmosphere 25-30 times faster than carbon dioxide. As the oceans warmed, the stores of frozen methane hydrate began melting, and methane gas rose to the atmosphere. Any remaining vegetation died, and with it, the last of the herbivores and carnivores.

By the end of the End-Permian mass extinction, 95% of all life had vanished, and it would take life on Earth around ten million years to fully recover from this extinction event that completely reset the evolutionary process. In the seas, ancestral crabs, lobsters, and the first marine reptiles began to thrive. Two important land species to survive the extinction were therapsids (ancestors of mammals) and archosaurs (ancestors of dinosaurs).

A group of therapsids—the cynodonts—small, rodent-like animals, learned to burrow underground to escape predators. This subterranean lifestyle proved advantageous since the Earth's surface remained subject to such high temperatures. Tubers, grubs, and plant roots provided sufficient nutrition and water for them to lead successful lives. These early ancestors of the first mammals were small, insectivorous, nocturnal, hairy, warm-blooded, and laid eggs. Today, we know of two primitive mammals that lay eggs: the platypus and the spiny anteater echidna.

Archosaurs are the ancestors of all dinosaurs, birds, and crocodilians. Archosaurs evolved during the Triassic period, as did petrosaurs, which became the first animals after insects to develop the ability to fly. Dinosaurs began their evolution around 230 million years ago as tiny bipedal predators, but after the fourth mass extinction, they grew larger with more specialized features, and ruled the Earth until roughly 65 million years ago.

Food for Thought

From our understanding of geology, an event similar to the one that took place in Siberia happens once every 100 million years. We need not worry about such a natural disaster occurring again, as we cannot do anything to prevent or prepare for it. However, a greater danger, one which we do have the potential to impede looms on the horizon—the devastating effects of human activities.

For the first time in history, Earth's dominant species has also come to represent its greatest threat, particularly due to our production of carbon dioxide. If we continue this way, over the next two centuries, we will release two to three thousand gigatons of carbon dioxide into the atmosphere, the same amount of carbon dioxide released from the Siberian traps roughly 252 million years ago.

The devastation of the End-Permian extinction event will most certainly be seen again if we continue to pollute the Earth, especially considering that we have trillions of tons of methane hydrate locked in ice at the bottom of our oceans. Because this gas is extremely sensitive to temperature change, an increase of just one or two degrees Celsius could destabilize it and release the stored methane hydrate, just as it did in the Permian oceans 252 million years ago, causing another runaway global warming event.

The Fourth Great Mass Extinction Event

The Triassic-Jurassic mass extinction occurred 201 million years ago, and wiped out 70-75% of the species in existence. It took about 10,000 years for this extinction to run its course, and there are three popular hypotheses among experts for its cause. Though it lacks strong scientific evidence, the first hypothesis places the blame on climate change and sea level fluctuations. The second hypothesis involves an asteroid impact, but no crater has ever been discovered that would be large enough to have caused such an extinction.

The third and most popular hypothesis is massive volcanic eruptions in the form of flood basalts. These explosions occurred at the Central Atlantic Magmatic Province (CAMP), a large magma flow that erupted 201 million years ago when the supercontinent Pangaea broke apart. A huge volcanic rift spewed magma out of the Earth, and split the Americas from Europe and Africa, forming the Atlantic Ocean. These eruptions would have blanketed the atmosphere with carbon dioxide and caused the global temperature increase that led to this annihilation event.

After the extinction, many of the archosaurs and large amphibians disappeared, paving the way for dinosaurs to become the apex predators. Over the next 135 million years, dinosaurs grew to enormous sizes and diversified into an amazing variety of shapes with specialized adaptations. Their planetary dominance was short-lived, however, since an extra-terrestrial body was on its way to exterminate the dinosaurs and give mammals a chance to take over.

The Fifth Great Mass Extinction Event

Sixty-five million years ago, at the end of the Cretaceous period, an asteroid collided with our planet, causing the Cretaceous-Paleogene mass extinction. The impact triggered a chain of events that eliminated 75% of all species on the planet, including the dinosaurs. This was one of the most significant and legendary events in the history of Earth—it provided solid proof of an asteroid striking our planet, ended the reign of the dinosaurs, and paved the way for the emergence of mammals and, eventually, humans.

Geologists and paleontologists discovered evidence for this extinction deep within the sedimentary rocks of the Cretaceous-Paleogene, or K-Pg boundary. This layer of the fossil record creates a geological border separating the reign of the dinosaurs from the time of their disappearance. Below this periphery, scientists discovered fossilized dinosaur bones, but there was no evidence of these animals ever existing above it. After careful analysis of the K-Pg boundary layer, scientists detected high levels of iridium, a rare metal on Earth, usually only found in the planet's core. However, iridium is highly common in meteors and asteroids, leading researchers to speculate whether or not an asteroid impact had caused the mass extinction.

Scientists estimated that for this asteroid to cause such a devastation, it must have been the size of Mount Everest, with an impact crater 100 miles (160 km) in diameter. They also speculated that iridium would have spread across the globe as it entered the atmosphere and returned to Earth's surface as rain. This was indeed found to be the case, since traces of iridium were discovered in the K-Pg layer in different geological sites across the world. Along with iridium, scientists found fragmented mineral crystals (quartz). Crystals in this condition are better known as shocked quartz, because their microscopic structures have been distorted on impact with an object traveling at speeds of thousands of miles per hour. There is only one natural phenomenon powerful enough to cause such damage to quartz—an asteroid collision—so researchers began searching for an impact zone.

In 1978, an oil company surveying the Yucatan peninsula stumbled upon a horse shoe-shaped configuration beneath the sea off the Mexican coast. Geophysical data and gravity field maps from the survey showed that this mysterious form was buried three-quarters of a mile (1.2 km) under the sea. It was 12 miles (19 km) deep, with an impact ring of 93 miles (150 km) in diameter. Drilling samples exhibited the same high levels of iridium and shocked quartz, matching the earlier samples found in the K-Pg boundary layer.

Experts theorize that 65 million years ago, an asteroid traveling at 45,000 miles per hour (72,000 km/hr) was headed straight for present-day Mexico. It was 6 miles (9.65 km) wide, 35,000 feet (10,668 m) high and weighed one trillion tons. It crashed into the sea at 60 times the speed of sound. Everything within a 1,000-mile (1,609 km) radius was instantly incinerated. To provide a concept of how massive this asteroid was, consider that the moment it touched the ground, its top edge would have reached 35,000 feet (10,668 m)—the altitude at which commercial airplanes generally fly.

Scientists specializing in asteroid impacts have recreated this collision in their labs at the NASA Ames

71

Research Center outside San Francisco. The Ames Vertical Gun can fire a projectile at 18,000 miles per hour (29,000 km/hr), and a scaled-down model is used to shoot a projectile into a pit of sand and water. The event is recorded using ultra-high-speed cameras, and scientists were thus able to calculate the effects of an asteroid of this size— a searing shockwave spread from the impact site at 2,000 miles per hour (3,219 km/hr), instantly reducing any nearby life to ashes. Five hundred billion tons of material shot into the atmosphere, and a 300-foot-high (91 m) mega tsunami launched across the Gulf of Mexico at hundreds of miles per hour, devastating the entire coastal region.

Researchers discovered approximately 70 billion tons of soot in the K-Pg boundary layer across the globe, indicating that the majority of vegetation on Earth had been incinerated. For several hours after the impact, billions of tons of super-heated debris rained down across the globe, setting the entire planet on fire. As roughly 500 tons of debris re-entered the Earth's atmosphere, the heat it produced caused spontaneous combustion across vast areas of vegetation. The majority of animals, including the dinosaurs, died in the global wildfires, but the species that survived the blazes did not outlive the resulting climate changes. The entire atmosphere became saturated with dust and ash from the wildfires, which prevented the sun's rays from reaching Earth for the next three to six months, and caused a dramatic decrease in global temperatures.

The lack of sunlight also led to the extinction of 70% of marine life, as plankton became scarce since it relied so heavily on sunlight. Many species that fed on plankton died, sparing only the creatures in the deepest oceans that were able to find alternative food sources. To make things worse, the geological landscape of the Yucatan peninsula contained an abundance of sulfurous minerals, which transferred tons of sulfur dioxide into the atmosphere during the blast. When combined with water, sulfur dioxide turned into sulfuric acid, which reflected the sun's rays to outer space and led the Earth's temperature to eventually drop by five degrees Celsius and cause a global winter. Ultimately, the sulfur dioxide fell back down to Earth in the form of acid rain, killing any plant life still struggling to survive. With their food sources depleted, the remaining animals faced starvation and eventually died.

As global cooling slowed and came to an end, global warming began again. Along with sulfur, the asteroid blast vaporized billions of tons of greenhouse gases into the atmosphere—the equivalent of 3,000 years of modern fossil fuel burning. This severe global warming lasted for several centuries, with temperatures shooting up 20 °C almost immediately. The world turned into a desert and the remaining plant-eating dinosaurs starved, leaving the carnivorous dinosaurs to the same fate. And as such, after 165 million years, the reign of the dinosaurs came to an end. The only dinosaurs to survive this catastrophe had the ability to fly, and would later evolve into birds. Frogs, turtles, and crocodiles also survived this extinction thanks to characteristics that suited their new environment, such as living or laying eggs underground.

It is truly extraordinary to contemplate the fact that were it not for this asteroid impact, dinosaurs would have continued to dominate the planet. Mammals would not have had the opportunity to diversify, and we would not be here to tell this amazing story. After 165 million years of complete dominance, the dinosaurs became obsolete. Humans have been on this planet for nearly 200,000 years, and a similar-sized asteroid is likely to collide with the Earth roughly every 100 million years. We ought to reflect on the fragility of human existence on this planet and understand that we, too, could become extinct in a single moment.

The Reign of Mammals

Initially evolving around 200 million years ago, and with dinosaurs out of the picture, mammals rose to prominence in this new environment. The mammals that survived the chaos were small, rodent-like creatures and their ability to burrow underground allowed them to escape the devastation on Earth's surface. As omnivores, they could eat a variety of foods such as plants, insects, and other small animals, giving them a better chance of survival than species with restricted diets.

Unlike cold-blooded reptiles, these warm-blooded mammals were less dependent on environmental temperatures, which allowed them to populate the colder regions of the world. Additionally, new habitats with plentiful food resources were available to exploit. As the Earth began to recover from the asteroid impact, flowering plants returned, providing sustenance for the rapidly-multiplying insects. In turn, fruits, berries, and insects became a high-quality food source for mammals, and sprouting forests offered them new habitats.

Within 10-15 million years of the extinction of dinosaurs, the number and diversity of mammals had sky-rocketed. There were around 4,000 or so species which included the first fully aquatic mammals (whales), flying mammals (bats), and rodents. Primates appeared roughly 65-55 million years ago, and some 48 million years later, upright-walking hominids evolved.

CHAPTER THREE

HUMAN ORIGINS

Human Origins

Thirty-five million years ago, the creation of the Great Rift Valley changed the course of evolution for a group of apes living in the trees of the African rainforests. This geological fracture split the African plains in two and formed a trench approximately 3,700 miles (6,000 km) wide, extending from present day Lebanon to Mozambique. The fissure created gigantic mountain ranges in central and western Africa, and winds carrying moisture and rain across the plains now faced a natural barrier. This caused a phenomenon known as a rain shadow, in which massive amounts of rain continued to fall on the western side of the mountains, but the eastern side experienced a drastic reduction in precipitation.

During the next millions of years, the eastern rainforests died out, and with fewer trees to sustain them, the apes descended to the forest floors in search of food. If this geological rift had not occurred on the African plains, humans would not exist as we do today. The savannah's climate would have remained unchanged, and apes would have continued living in trees rather than adapting to walk upright on two legs. The succession of events that led to the arrival of modern humans onto the evolutionary scene occurred over a period of seven million years, and describes the journey of how we came to be the only species of upright-walking hominids in existence today.

Bipedalism

As humans, one of our most unique traits is the ability to walk upright on two legs. Although some apes are capable of this feat for short durations, humans are the only mammals to walk on two legs throughout the course of their entire lives. Since we are the only species in existence to do so today, it is difficult to investigate how this behavior began, but experts have formulated two hypotheses.

The first hypothesis suggests that as apes descended to the ground, it became increasingly difficult for them to find food, especially for females raising offspring. Males took on the role of gathering food to feed their families, and the females rewarded this behavior with exclusive mating. The males needed their arms free to carry their loot back to their families as well as protect it from competitors, and this behavior led to the evolution of bipedalism.

The second hypothesis proposes that walking on two legs conserved critical energy. When lab-tested, the energy consumption of a chimp walking on four legs was four times more than that of humans walking on two legs. As the forests shrank, these apes were forced to travel longer distances between trees in search of food. Walking on four legs is extremely energy-consuming for chimpanzees and apes because their bodies are built for climbing trees. Adapting to life on the ground required the apes to walk upright, enabling them to conserve energy and cover more ground. Regardless of the cause of bipedal evolution in apes, this anatomical change did not occur over a few generations, but took thousands and thousands of years.

In order to approximate when the divergence between apes and humans took place, researchers depend upon a technique known as the molecular clock, which enables them to compare DNA from closely-related species to determine the amount of time that had elapsed since their divergence. This method is based on the constant rate of change in DNA sequencing, because a new species typically evolves when DNA spontaneously creates a variation while copying itself. These changes are referred to as mutations; most are deadly or inhibitive, but those that prove beneficial are passed on to the next generations. By counting the differences between the genetic codes of apes and humans, scientist determined that the first evolutionary step between the two species took place around seven million years ago. Examining several of the most famous fossil finds that led to *Homo sapiens* will shed a bit of light on our own evolution.

In 2001, scientists discovered a peculiar skull, named Toumai, which carbon dated to roughly seven million years ago in norther Chad. Experts believe this *Sahelanthropus tchadensis* may have been the first species to diverge from apes on the journey of human evolution. In order to unlock the secrets of this skull, scientists needed to first reconstruct it, a task that was undertaken in Grenoble,

France with the aid of a particle accelerator. This powerful X-ray scanner took more than 1,000 pictures to create a 3-D model of the skull, and experts used these virtual images to restore the skull to its original shape using a 3-D printer.

The crucial question was whether or not Toumai walked upright on two legs, and the answer to this lay in the manner in which the skull attached to the spine. When the skull was placed on a spine of an ape that walked on four legs, the eyes pointed downward, verifying that such a creature could not have walked on four legs because it would have been unable to see directly ahead of itself to avoid predators or find food. However, when the skull was set onto the skeleton of a biped, the eyes pointed forward, leading most scientists to conclude that Toumai was indeed an upright walker. Over the next seven million years, multiple bipedal species with chimp-like brains evolved and exhibited very few differences from each other:

- *Orrorin tugenensis* (6.1-5.7 million years ago)
- *Ardipithecus ramidus* (5.8-4.4 million years ago)
- *Kenyanthropus platyops* (3.5-3.2 million years ago)
- *Australopithecus afarensis* (3.9-2.9 million years ago)

In 2000, researchers working in Dikika, Ethiopia unearthed a small skull that appeared similar to that of a baby chimp, but several peculiarities distinguished it from other known samples. The skull rested just above white bands of volcanic ash which dated to 3.4 million years ago,

80

and was therefore estimated to be approximately 3.3 million years old. The baby, named Salam, belonged to *Australopithecus afarensis*, the same species as Lucy, the famous fossil discovered in the 1970s.

Interestingly, Salam and Lucy presented both ape and human features. Salam's skull had been fossilized by sandstone; scientist worked for eight years to remove the grit and expose the underlying bone—a truly amazing feat, considering the delicacy and precision this task required. To determine her age at the time of Salam's death, scientists examined her teeth with CT scans. The scans showed intact adult teeth in her gums; thus she was only three-years-old when she died. By analyzing her skeletal remains, researchers determined that Salam—like Lucy—walked upright, due to the orientation of her hip bones and the articulation of the knee joint along the pelvis. From the waist down, Salam and Lucy showed human traits, but exhibited more ape-like characteristics from the waist up. These creatures most likely slept in trees at night for protection and walked upright during the day as they foraged for food.

The scientists who sought to understand Salam's thought process studied her brain, which was 75% formed at the time of her death, according to fossil comparisons with her species. A chimp's brain is fully developed by age three, while a human brain takes approximately 20 years to mature, and this variance in the duration of childhood is the main difference between modern man and ape. Researchers comparing the human brain to our closest relative—the chimpanzee—searched for signs of evolution in the folds and creases of the brain's surface. The most important structure to examine is the lunate sulcus, a fissure deep in a primate's brain which divides the neocortex—the area responsible for complex thinking—from its components related to vision. The human brain does not have as deep a crease as does a chimp, and the neocortex is larger than the vision component located at the back of the brain. The reconstruction of Salam's skull enabled researchers to study her brain's structures by making an endocast, a casting technique that preserves the impression of the brain's surface inside the skull.

When Salam's endocast was compared to that of a chimp, paleo-neurologists noticed the lunate sulcus had shifted toward the back of the brain, allowing room for a larger neocortex, which indicated that Salam and members of her species were more intelligent than an ordinary chimp. Although relatively the same size as that of a chimp, the brain of *Australopithecus afarensis* had been rewired to make room for more advanced thinking. This enabled Salam's species to extend their duration of childhood, which gave them more time to learn the advanced skills associated with communal living and the bipedal search for food. By contrast, a chimp's brain is fully developed by the age of three because life in the trees does not demand the same level of complex thought process as it does on the ground.

Homo Habilis

Approximately three million years ago, glaciers spreading across the globe locked the majority of Earth's water in its poles. The glaciers subsequently receded, drawing moisture toward the equator, and as this process repeated itself for hundreds of thousands of years, massive climate fluctuations forced the hominids to adapt or die. Consequently, scientists examining the sedimentary rock layers pertaining to this time period found something they had never seen before—rocks that had been shaped by hominids and used as stone tools. Researchers emphasized that these were not ordinary rocks, but had been purposefully and methodically formed because they had been broken in a particular manner, with the sides trimmed away to create a sharper edge. *Homo habilis* lived between 2.4 and 1.5 million years ago, and used these stone tools to crack the long bones of animals in order to reach the nutritious marrow deep within. Many types of broken bones with clear-cut marks including turtles, crocodiles, antelopes, and even hippopotami were found in the areas where this species resided.

These findings also mark the onset of a primarily carnivorous diet, an important stage in human development which helped us meet the increased energy demands that came with a larger brain. The hand bones of *Homo habilis* show a thumb similar to our own, built to employ a precise grip and provide the required dexterity to shape and make use of stone tools. *Homo habilis* stood only three to four feet (90-120 cm) tall, but had a larger brain than all the bipeds that preceded him in the previous five million years. The elevated, sloped forehead of *Homo habilis* indicated an expansion in the frontal lobe where higher levels of cognition and reasoning take place. The brain size nearly doubled from 24.5 inches^3 (400 cm^3) in *Australopithecus afarensis* to 43-39 inches^3 (700-800 cm^3) in *Homo habilis*. With the features of *Homo habilis* resembling humans rather than apes, we can recognize the face of our own species beginning to emerge.

Scientists spent many years searching for clues to explain why human evolution kick-started with *Homo habilis*, especially since the brain size of previous hominids remained roughly the same. Layers of rock dating back to the evolution of *Homo habilis* paint a picture of a continuously transforming landscape: lakes appeared and disappeared, volcanoes erupted violently, and desertification occurred rapidly. The need to survive turbulent climates and environmental changes forced these species to adapt or face extinction.

Researchers studied these climate fluctuations by examining layers of deep sea sediment drilled from the ocean floor. The sediments, which accumulate slowly and continuously over time, are composed of dust that subsequently lands at the bottom of the ocean. In this way, experts are able to determine that variations in the sediment layers reflect the amount of precipitation that occured, providing them with an approximation of the weather at the time. If the dust layer appears thick, that means it was easily picked up and dispersed by the wind, indicating a dry climate. In contrast, a thin layer indicates a greater amount of rainfall for that particular period. To approximate when this dust was blown into the ocean, scientists investigated shells of microscopic sea creatures embedded in these layers. After an extensive analysis, the results showed that in the three to four million years prior to the existence of *Homo habilis*, the weather in Africa remained relatively stable and dry, but 200,000 years of extreme climate variations followed. As the brain of *Homo habilis* evolved to adapt to this new environment, we see stone tools beginning to appear in the fossil records. Multiple bipedal species faced climate instability, and those unable to adapt—such as Lucy and Salam—died, while skilled problem-solvers like *Homo habilis* survived. Microclimate change is currently the most widely-accepted hypothesis to explain the further evolution of these hominids approximately two million years ago.

Homo Erectus

Turbulent climate fluctuations continued for another million and a half years, during which time many other *Homo* species adapted and evolved complex thought processes and survival mechanisms in order to adjust to their ever-changing environment.

One of these creatures, *Homo erectus,* evolved in the Great Rift Valley of East Africa two million years ago. This species appeared more human than ape, exhibiting a larger brain, longer legs, and thinner arms than the preceding hominids. *Homo erectus* was an accomplished hunter and tool-maker who achieved the greatest evolutionary leap between humans and apes. This is the time when the human traits of creativity, intelligence, and compassion begin to emerge.

In 1984, paleoanthropologists in Lake Turkana in northern Kenya discovered a male *Homo erectus* skeleton and named him Turkana Boy. At 1.5 million years old and almost fully complete, he was certainly a rare find. Turkana Boy was 5.3 feet (160 cm) tall, with a physical build resembling a man more than an ape. To determine his age, scientists studied the growth plates on his limbs, which had not fused as they would have in an adult male, indicating that Turkana Boy had been growing at the time of his death. Dental specialists also examined the fossilized teeth to approximate his age using a remarkable technique. An enamel cap made of dentin—otherwise known as ivory—covers the core of the tooth, and creates a growth pattern like the rings of a tree. Within these rings, rods comprised of cells resembling tiny beads run from the core to the surface of the tooth. Because the circadian rhythm influences the cells that produce enamel, each bead represents one day of growth. These secretions, which speed up during the day and slow at night, are recorded within the tooth and are observable under an extremely powerful electron microscope. Counting the number of beads in the rods of the tooth enamel enables scientists to approximate the age of an individual.

After careful analysis of Turkana Boy's teeth, researchers determined that he was eight years old at the time of his death, implying that his growth rate was more like chimpanzees than humans. Chimpanzees reach sexual maturity at age seven, while humans become sexually mature after approximately 12 years. In relation to body size, the human brain is the largest among the mammals, and therefore requires additional growth outside the womb, otherwise our heads would never be able to pass through the birth canal. A long childhood allows the brain to develop and grow as we learn how to function in our complex societies. With a brain size of 55 inches^3 (900 cm^3), the endocast of Turkana Boy's skull revealed that his Broca's area seemed more developed, which indicated that he likely utilized representational communication skills such as gesturing. It is difficult to determine if Turkana Boy was able to speak, but his use of tools demonstrated a higher level of intelligence than his predecessors.

Our modern brains consume 20-25% of the body's energy supply, and this was also the case for early members of *Homo erectus*. The species required high-calorie meals with a great deal of fat and protein in order to survive, but since *Homo erectus* lacked the speed or strength to tackle large animals, they needed to devise alternate strategies to catch their meal. The most important adaptation for covering long distances without rest is the ability to sweat as a means of cooling the body. Since *Homo erectus* did not have a full coat of hair or fur, they were able to perspire freely, which greatly improved their endurance. Many animals on the African savanna display remarkable speed when travelling short distances, but require rest in order to release the heat from their bodies soon afterward. By contrast, *Homo erectus* and *Homo sapiens* are capable of running entire marathons without respite.

We know that *Homo erectus* lost the majority of its fur coat by examining the lice that was present on their bodies. A single variety typically plagues most creatures, but as a result of the hairless barrier between our heads and genitals, two different types feed on humans: pubic lice and head lice. However, when early *Homo sapiens* began losing their body hair, the pests migrated toward their heads, and when our ancestors came into contact with gorillas—perhaps while scavenging their bodies for meat or sleeping in their abandoned caves—lice from the apes latched onto their pubic hair. It appears that our pubic lice are closely related to those found on gorillas, and by determining exactly when these two species of lice diverged from one another, researchers were able to approximate the time when humans lost their body hair.

Using the molecular genetic clock, scientists discovered these two species of lice shared a common ancestor as recently as three million years ago, and that two million years ago, *Homo erectus* had very little body hair. This feature allowed the species to pursue prey for long distances in the heat of the mid-day sun. The ability to sweat was the key to the survival and evolution of the species, since quadrupeds are only able to run for 10-15 minutes at a time. *Homo erectus* exploited this advantage by pursuing their prey to the point of exhaustion, until hunters could get close enough to use clubs, rocks, or short-distance spears to kill their next meal. This method, known as persistence hunting, continues to be practiced by several African societies today, including the Bushmen of the Kalahari Tribe.

Homo erectus was also the first hominid to tame fire, which allowed for the physical and social evolution of the species. Heating food made it softer and easier to digest, and also explains why *Homo erectus* developed smaller teeth and stomachs than their predecessors. With numerous nocturnal predators on the African savanna, *Homo erectus* required fire for protection, and cooking rituals also served to greatly improve social behavior as members of this species learned to communicate and share resources while dining.

The incredible discovery of a *Homo erectus* jaw belonging to an old man who had lost his teeth two years prior to his death confirmed their newfound sense of community. This find indicated that someone had fed this man or even chewed his food for him, demonstrating an emotional maturity in the social life of *Homo erectus*. The most important legacy of this species was the instinct to cooperate with and care for other members of their social groups.

In addition to an increased sense of compassion, *Homo erectus* was the first species of biped to leave Africa, and it appears these migrations began approximately 1.9 million years ago. These relocations were the result of environmental changes that affected the availability of food and natural resources. As grassy lands spread from Africa into Asia, game animals and *Homo erectus* followed. It was likely a slow migration with different groups traveling only one or two kilometers annually. One million years after their departure from the African plains, *Homo erectus* had spread throughout Asia and Europe. Experts discovered fossil evidence of *Homo erectus* in Asia dating as recently as 108,000 years ago, testifying to the remarkable perseverance and adaptive skills of a species that survived for two million years.

Neanderthals

All other types of hominids evolved from *Homo erectus*, and one species, *Homo heidelbergensis*, gave rise to *Homo neanderthalensis* in Europe and *Homo sapiens* in Africa. More commonly referred to as Neanderthals, *Homo neanderthalensis* appeared in Europe approximately 430,000 years ago, and due to the short, stocky bodies which helped them survive multiple ice ages, this ancestor most closely resembles modern humans.

The first Neanderthal skull—named Engis 2—was discovered in 1829, when the idea of evolution was quite unpopular. Therefore, scientists examining these fossils assumed that Neanderthals were diseased or deformed humans instead of an entirely separate species. Neanderthals built and employed sophisticated tools, assembled and wore clothing, lived in caves, manipulated fire, and were skilled hunters of large animals. They also consumed plants, crafted decorative objects, and might have believed in appeasing an after-death medium, as evidenced by burial of their dead and the discoveries of ornamental offerings at grave sites.

By examining their endocasts, researchers determined that the frontal lobe of Neanderthals is almost identical to our own. However, Neanderthals exhibited smaller parietal and temporal lobes, suggesting limited mental capacity, as these parts of the brain control cognition, language, memory, and the ability to remember and return to specific locations.

In order to determine the diet of the Neanderthals, scientists studied the composition of their bones, since consumed food leaves unique traces inside the proteins. Based on this analysis, Neanderthals subsisted almost entirely on meat, and bones tested across Europe yielded similar results. The simplicity of their weapons made tracking and hunting prey an extremely dangerous task. Trackers still needed to come rather close to kill larger animals, so it comes as no surprise that the majority of male Neanderthal skeletons found in Europe exhibited multiple fractures. Neanderthals led harsh lives, and very few lived beyond the age of 30, yet the species sustained itself for

400,000 years—twice as long as modern humans—before vanishing from the fossil record 40,000 years ago.

Homo sapiens

Roughly 200,000 years ago, *Homo sapiens* evolved from *Homo heidelbergensis* in the Great Rift Valley of Africa. The oldest *Homo sapiens* fossil unearthed thus far was discovered in Omo, Ethiopia and dates back to 195,000 years ago. As drought and desertification spread across Africa, the majority of *Homo sapiens* died, while the remainder were forced to survive in highlands or near the sea, and our species came to the brink of extinction when our numbers dwindled to just 600 individuals in Africa. Because we are all descendants of these 600 individuals, the genetic composition of humans today is 99.99% identical. This population, which gave rise to the rest of our species, made their home on the South African coastline, and employed innovative means of navigating tides to collect shellfish as well as engineered intricate tools to improve fishing techniques. With the ability to adapt to their ever-changing surroundings came an increased interest in the patterns of the natural world.

Roughly 82,000 years ago, we see the first instances of artistry with small perforated seashell beads used for personal adornment. The first evidence of decorative art also appears around this time, in the form of cave paintings with red ochre, a naturally occurring mineral found on the South African coast. These humans began to assign abstract meaning to the patterns and elements of nature that surrounded them, and also started using symbols to record information that could be passed on to future generations.

Fossil evidence dating back 71,000 years shows that early humans made great advancements in tool production by constructing specialized utensils to suit specific tasks: sharp spears designed to kill and flatter hand instruments for carving or scraping. Forging these tools in fire increased their strength and allowed us to take full advantage of our environment. For example, the invention of the bow and arrow some 64,000 years ago greatly decreased the danger involved in hunting, and provided *Homo sapiens* with the high calorie intake they required for successful adaptation and survival.

By relying upon the molecular clock technique to examine the evolution of lice in clothing samples, researchers approximate that humans began wearing clothes roughly 170,000 years ago. Thanks to new technologies, the ability to form social groups, and warm clothing, the first modern humans began migrating out of Africa into the colder climates of Europe and Asia between 70,000 and 50,000 years ago.

As the populations of *Homo sapiens* grew in Europe, they directly competed with the Neanderthals for food and resources, eventually pushing them to extinction. *Homo sapiens* were capable of using more advanced technology, not to mention being physically taller, faster, and stronger. Furthermore, the metabolic systems of the Neanderthals needed approximately 5,000 calories a day while *Homo sapiens* could subsist on less than half that amount. *Homo sapiens* also utilized throwing spears and bows and arrows to hunt, which were skills the Neanderthals lacked, giving *Homo sapiens* a much greater advantage in their ecological niche. The last traces of Neanderthals were discovered 40,000 years ago, signifying that for the first time in history, *Homo sapiens* were the only species of hominids on the planet. These innovative humans reached Asia and the Middle East roughly 10,000 years after first migrating out of Africa, and between five and ten thousand years after that, several of these early populations made the 56-mile (90 km) journey from Indonesia to Australia on open water, meaning they possessed the ingenuity and innovation to construct some type of boats. As such, with the exception of Antarctica, humans populated all of Earth's continents in a relatively short amount of time. Scientists have been able to determine the movements of our species across the world by studying the extinctions of large animals. Our arrival in Europe and Asia coincides with the disappearance of wooly mammoths, cave lions, and similar enormous mammals, since the ability to hunt large game ensured the survival of the species. In Australia, the majority of animals that weighed more than 100 pounds (45 kg) disappeared within a few thousand years of our arrival.

Another factor affecting these migration and settlement patterns was the cultivation of crops approximately 10,000 years ago. No longer dependent on migrating herds for sustenance, humans could now remain in the same location for longer and longer periods of time. Since agricultural practices and the domestication of local animals could supply plenty of sustenance for the rapidly-growing populations, permanent settlements gradually came to replace the nomadic way of life for many tribes. Humans began to form distinct groups that differentiated them from one another geographically, culturally, linguistically, and even genetically. These early civilizations offered communal bonds, protection, instruction for acceptable behavior, and in essence, shaped our view of the entire world.

However, as centuries passed, these primitive social groupings grew into behemoth societies, which have now completely removed us from nature both physically and mentally, and placed us in concrete jungles that offer only the occasional glimpse of nature. This division causes us to think and operate as though we are separate from nature, but if one takes just a moment to consider the sun that gives all species life, the food we eat and the water we drink, the ground upon which we stand and the air we breathe, surely we can realize that we do indeed belong to the natural world.

Sadly, such thoughts do not often cross our minds, as we tend to live our lives without any real knowledge or appreciation of the origin of the universe, the planet we live on, or the evolution of life that brought us into existence. So many of us merely live in a falsely-constructed reality, cycling through the same motions every day, completely unaware that we support a global structure of inequality, corruption, and greed. As this system destroys us mentally and physically, it also blinds us to our obvious connection to nature and even affects our sense of humanity, both as individuals and within the larger social context. I believe there are two main reasons behind this destructive and maddening facade: organized religion and the financial system.

CHAPTER FOUR

GODS AND RELIGIONS

Gods and Religions

The concept of a higher power has been an integral part of human awareness since the beginning of our evolution, and though it has proven beneficial to our survival at times, believing in a supernatural entity now represents a detrimental part of our cognitive process. Our earliest religious beliefs began with the realization that certain variables in nature such as predators, diseases, and natural disasters threatened our survival, while other phenomenon such as the sun and rain contributed to our prosperity. Since we did not understand the reasons for these natural occurrences, we began to assign significance to them, and two separate mechanisms of our cognitive process emerged to explain these phenomena: religious doctrine and scientific inquiry.

When *Homo sapiens* first appeared some 200,000 years ago, we adopted the beliefs of our ancestors, which had been developing for the last seven million years. As depicted by fossilized tools, our scientific thinking capabilities were still quite primitive at that time, so it is easy to see why an innate curiosity coupled with a limited understanding of their environment led early humans to concoct their own explanations of natural phenomena in order to make sense of their surroundings.

Another key point of discussion is a psychological mechanism inherited from our ancestors that helped us survive in the wild. Imagine yourself as a hominid on the plains of Africa several million years ago. You hear a rustle in the grass behind you—is it a dangerous predator, or simply a gust of wind? If you assumed the noise was a threat, but it turned out to be simply the breeze, you have just made a relatively harmless mistake known as a type one error, a false positive error. On the other hand, if you believed the rustling noise to be the wind in the grass, and it turned out to be a predator, you have made a type two error, a false negative error, which likely resulted in death.

Modern humans descended from hominids who consistently made type one errors, since those inclined to make type two errors tended to be less cautious than their peers and did not often survive long enough to reproduce. As such, from a very early stage in our evolution, our brains were programmed to believe that there is something or someone behind all the natural occurrences that surrounded us. Assigning intentional agents or personifications to environmental features such as the sun, moon, wind, lightning, rain, and volcanoes marked the origin of our superstitious belief in deities of nature. The primitive mind evolved various forms of worship in an attempt to appease these intentional agents so as to alleviate the fear of negative occurrences such as starvation, infection, and disease, or even "prevent" them.

Another component of our supernatural beliefs is the understanding that one day our lives will come to an end. With this realization, the human mind constructed the possibility of living beyond the physical world, providing a reassuring narrative to help us accept the fact the we will eventually die. It is possible that we were born with a mechanism in our brain which allows us to believe in the duality of existence, as it seems to be evolutionarily advantageous to acquire such a trait, or else the crippling fear of awaiting our death would have inhibited the chances of our survival.

The belief that a higher power controls our lives largely originated from our ignorance of the natural world. As our species began to expand and migrate, early humans met with an increasing number of new and potentially dangerous situations. These encounters gave our primitive ancestors the incentive to continually create new gods to appease when facing social or environmental challenges. The variety of gods and religions throughout history demonstrates that humans drew inspiration directly from whatever natural elements surrounded them at the time to construct these deities, rituals, and beliefs.

Remarkably, only minor cellular adaptations have taken place since the onset of human evolution, thus there are no real biological differences between a person living today and one from 200,000 years ago—only our way of thinking has evolved and improved over time. We must also recognize that the information our ancestors accumulated about the unknown natural phenomena around them was passed on to the next generations regardless of accuracy. If our predecessors had possessed the scientific knowledge of the natural world that we do today, many of their religious beliefs would have quickly faded into obscurity. Fast-forward to modern times, where concrete evidence has largely replaced the mystery of ordinary occurrences in nature, and we can see that most of the religions human beings created to make sense of the unknown have disappeared long ago, and the majority of followers around the world now practice a monotheistic religion.

The monotheistic Abrahamic faiths are presently the most popular, and all stem from the Middle Eastern region: Judaism (around 4,000 years ago), Christianity (roughly 2,000 years ago), and Islam (approximately 1,400 years ago). Christianity and Islam are the two most widely-practiced religions, encompassing approximately four billion followers (2.2 billion Christians and 1.8 billion Muslims). Of course, there are many other religions in the world today—nearly 4,200 in total—but a large portion of humanity has adopted one of these two. Though these religions all speak of the same God and His prophets, they have also caused and continue to cause the most hatred, division, and destruction in the world.

It is worth noting that many ancestors of the adherents to these religions had these beliefs forced upon them. For example, Christianity was first adopted by the Roman Empire in the fourth century, and spread across Europe by means of conquest. Similarly, Islam took over most of the Middle East, the Iberian Peninsula, and regions of Asia and Africa during the seventh century. Europeans exported Christianity to South and North America, Australia, and parts of Africa and Asia, also through war and subjugation.

For this discussion, I shall refer to the King James version of the Old and New Testaments of the Bible, and all passages referenced come from a basic English version that can be found on O-bible.com. Though I have also read the Quran, which describes the same Abrahamic God and prophets presented in the Bible, I will abstain from discussing it, because if I were to openly criticize Islam, I would fear for the safety of my family in Lebanon. Instead, I shall focus my critiques on the supernatural and moral claims of the Old and New Testaments, as these represent the main pillars of Christianity, Judaism, and Islam. Nevertheless, I do advise reading both the Bible and the Quran, because the majority of people who believe in the Abrahamic God have not personally read these books, and therefore do not know how far-fetched and bizarre they actually are.

The Old Testament

The first chapters of Genesis tell us that God created the universe and the Earth in six days from nothing, a feat which some people believe took place as recently as 6,000-10,000 years ago. God then makes the first man, Adam, from the dust of the Earth, and the first woman, Eve, from his rib. God places them in the Garden of Eden, and allows them to eat the fruit of any tree except for the tree of knowledge of good and evil. A snake endowed with the power of speech convinces Eve to eat the fruit from this forbidden tree, which she later shares with Adam. When God discovers what they have done, He banishes Adam and Eve from the Garden of Eden, leaving them to fend for themselves. God curses Adam and Eve for their disobedience, and the Bible explains that this act of defiance is the reason their descendants must endure lives of suffering. The Bible also states that Adam lives to be 930 years old.

Several generations later, in the subsequent chapters of Genesis, God decides to kill everything on Earth with a flood. A man named Noah, his wife, their three sons, and their wives are the only people God chooses to survive this catastrophe. He instructs them to build a huge ark, and fill it with one male and one female from every species on Earth, leaving everything else on the planet to die. After the flood subsides, the animals from the boat and these eight individuals supposedly repopulate the entire planet, while Noah lives to the ripe old age of 950.

All logical evidence points to these being fictional stories fabricated by men: the universe is 13.8 billion years old, the Earth is 4.6 billion years old, humans evolved on this planet 200,000 years ago, snakes do not talk, and no evidence of a global flood has ever been found in the geological record, not to mention that no one lives to be 900 years old. For me, the story of this God begins and ends with these claims that directly contradict everything we know about the physical laws of the world in which we live.

In the narrative of Sodom and Gomorrah—cities teeming with people committing evil sins—God sends two angels to save one family from death. The angels tell Lot, his wife, and their two daughters to leave the town, warning them not to look back as God destroys the towns. God sends fire and flaming smoke to annihilate Sodom and Gomorrah, but during the escape, Lot's wife looks over her shoulder and is turned into a pillar of salt. Thereafter, Lot's daughters decide to get their father drunk with wine on two consecutive nights, so that each girl could have sex with him for the purpose of bearing more children. Genesis chapters 18-19 show us that God clearly does not object to any part of this disgusting deed, since each daughter later gives birth to a son fathered by Lot.

The narrative of Moses unfolds throughout the many chapters of Exodus, but one of the most notable occurrences is his discovery of a burning bush from which God speaks. God informs Moses that He has chosen him to lead the Children of Israel out of Egypt where they have been enslaved. This plan involves Moses and his brother, Aaron, visiting the Pharaoh to demand that he release the Israelites. At the same time, God warns Moses that He will harden the Pharaoh's heart so that he will refuse their request. Since the meeting does little to change the Pharaoh's mind, Aaron sets his staff on the ground and God turns it into a snake. The following day, Moses and Aaron visit the Pharaoh again, this time along the Nile River. Aaron places his rod over the river and turns the water into blood, instantly killing the fish and causing a putrid smell; even the water already stored in people's homes turns to blood. The following week, the Pharaoh refuses once again, so using his magic rod, Aaron initiates an outbreak of frogs from the Nile River. Next, God tells Aaron to touch the Earth with his staff, and all the grains of dust in Egypt are transformed into insects, devastating the land, except where the Children of Israel lived. In the following plague, God kills all the cattle owned by Egyptians and spares the cattle that belonged to the Children of Israel.

On the next visit, God commands Moses and Aaron to bring ashes from their fire and shower it before the

Pharaoh's eyes, and as they do, the dust spreads across the land, plaguing the Egyptians and their animals with a painful skin disease. Moses then lifts his staff to the sky, causing a fire and ice storm to simultaneously descend upon Egypt, crushing every tree and plant, except of course, those in the land where the Children of Israel lived. God then sends swarms of locusts to destroy any vegetation that may have survived, as well as three days of darkness to really get the Pharaoh thinking. In the final plague, God orders His people to kill a lamb and mark the top and sides of their doors with its blood, and then remain inside their homes. In the middle of the night, God's angel passes over the houses with lamb's blood on them, so the Children of Israel and their cattle remain unharmed yet again, while God kills the first-born male child of every family in Egypt, human or animal. And of course, we cannot forget the famous miracle of Exodus 14 in which the Pharaoh finally releases the Israelites from Egypt, but later sends his armies to recapture them. In order to escape, Moses parts the Red Sea by raising his staff, and then sends the waters crashing down onto the pursuing Egyptians once the Israelites have safely reached the opposite shore.

These chapters bring to mind an endless number of questions: What have the Egyptian families done to deserve God murdering their first-born males? If God needs to kill a child as some sort of gruesome punishment, should it not

107

only be the child of the man He intends to chastise? Why does God decide that all Egyptians must suffer for the actions of one man, especially when God controlled his actions in the first place?

As a young boy, I believed the narrative of Samson, found in Judges chapters 13-16, to be a fictional cartoon, but was shocked to recently discover that many believers consider it true, since it comes from the Bible. The story begins with God allowing the Philistines to enslave the Children of Israel for 40 years, since they have committed evil in his eyes. God sends an angel to appear before a married woman to inform her that she will soon give birth to a son whom he has chosen to free the Israelites. The angel instructs her never to cut the child's hair, and she gives birth to a boy named Samson, who grows to possess Herculean strength when he reaches adulthood.

The Bible tells of Samson once killing a lion with his bare hands as well as using the jawbone of an ass to kill 1,000 men in a single battle. Samson later falls in love with a woman named Delilah, and the Philistines offer her money to find the source of his strength. When Delilah discovers that his strength comes from his long hair, and Samson falls asleep on her knee, she calls for a man to cut it off. She then delivers him to the Philistines, who gouge out his eyes and imprison him in Gaza. The Philistinian lords hold a huge celebration with Samson tied between the two pillars of the house in order to ridicule their prisoner. Samson prays for God to give him strength one last time and allow him to die with the Philistines. God grants his wish, and Samson topples the pillars, killing himself and everyone else in the process. The story claims that he killed more people on that solitary day than throughout his entire life, including the incident with the jawbone. I cannot decide if this part of the story sounds more ridiculous than does possessing superhuman strength contingent on the length of one's hair.

2 Kings chapter 2 tells of Elisha and his master Elijah traveling throughout Palestine. When they arrive at the River Jordan, Elijah removes his robe, rolls it into a tube, and blows onto the water, parting it so that the men can walk on dry land, an accomplishment which sounds remarkably similar, yet no less plausible than the one performed by Moses at the Red Sea. Subsequently, a horse and carriage made of fire sweep Elijah up to Heaven in a great gust of wind, but do either of these incidents sound believable? Later in this remarkable story, Elisha arrives in a neighboring town where a group of children ridicule him for his baldness. Elisha curses them in the name of the Lord, and two bears instantly emerge from the nearby woods and kill the 42 offending youngsters. Does God really find a sense of justice in the murder of small children for teasing an adult who ought to be unaffected by their mockery? Can you

imagine the pain and agony they must have gone through for a bit of juvenile entertainment?

In Daniel chapter 3, King Nebuchadnezzar decides to burn three men from the Children of Israel (Shadrach, Meshach, and Abednego) because they refused to worship him and his gods. The king places them in a furnace, but they remain entirely uninjured throughout the entire ordeal—not even their clothes were damaged. Can you imagine that any believers would be willing to take a similar test in this day and age?

In the first two chapters of the book of Jonah, Jonah refuses an order from God and tries to run away from him. He boards a ship to the city of Tarshish, but God sends a violent storm over the sea. When the sailors realize Jonah is at fault, they throw him overboard, and the storm passes immediately. God then commands a huge fish to swallow Jonah for a duration of three days and three nights. Jonah prays to God, who eventually orders the fish to release him onto dry land. Is it really possible for a fish to consume an entire live human, only to spit him up three days later completely unharmed?

Much like the Old Testament, the New Testament is rife with tall tales of fantastic feats carried out by God's "chosen people." As we logically examine several of these accounts, it is difficult to say which testament contains the majority of these far-fetched narratives, but I suppose it is of little importance overall. As previously mentioned, it is more advantageous to simply rely upon your own reasoning and research as you genuinely question the validity of each example.

The New Testament

The New Testament begins with the virgin birth, wherein Mary is impregnated by the Holy Spirit. If a woman today claimed that she had magically become pregnant because an angel told her that she is carrying the Son of God, would you believe her? A million doctors could examine this woman, and I guarantee that not one of them would be able to declare her both pregnant *and* a virgin. Artificially inseminated by a medical professional, perhaps, but certainly not because of an angel's message. In my opinion, this discrepancy settles the matter quite clearly, yet in the second chapter of Matthew, we find a virgin mother giving birth to Jesus. Herod, the King of Jerusalem at the time, realizes that he may face some competition in the future, since it has been foretold that Jesus will become King of the Jews. Herod subsequently orders his men to kill all male children less than two years old in and around Bethlehem—did God allow so many innocent babies to die for the sake of just one?

In Matthew 3:17, as John the Baptist baptizes Jesus in the River Jordan, the Spirit of God comes to Jesus as a dove and a voice from Heaven says: "This is My Only Son Whom I love and with Whom I am well-pleased." Why did a similar voice not stop the United States from dropping atomic bombs on Japan or prevent countless other catastrophic events that resulted in the loss of innocent human lives? Would preventing such atrocities not have been a more appropriate time for God's voice to come out of the sky? In the following chapter, we find Jesus going without food or water for 40 days and 40 nights when he is tested by the devil in the desert—how long do you honestly think a human could survive in those conditions? Matthew chapters eight and nine feature more of the unlikely miracles that Jesus regularly performed, including ordering the wind and the sea to become calm in the middle of a storm, bringing various people back from the dead, and instantly healing paralyzed or blind individuals, but do any of these scenarios sound remotely believable?

In Matthew chapter 14, Jesus uses five loaves of bread and two fish to feed 5,000 men, women, and children, but where is he to give bread and fish to the millions of people who are deprived of food today? When the disciples depart from this magical picnic in a boat and encounter such violent winds that they fear for their lives, Jesus walks out upon the surface of the sea to help them. The disciples doubt it is truly him and Peter also attempts to walk upon the water, but calls out for Jesus when he finds himself sinking.

Jesus takes Peter's hand and when they return to the boat, the wind mysteriously stops, and everyone lives happily ever after. Can anyone really walk on water in a violent sea, let alone enable another person to do so?

In Matthew 24:34, Jesus declares that the end of the world will take place before the death of his disciples: "Truly, I say to you, this generation will not come to an end till all these things are complete," referring to the prediction in Matthew 24:29 of the sun darkening and the stars falling to Earth. According to Jesus, the Apocalypse was supposed to occur more than 2,000 years ago, and yet, here we are. In the second chapter of John, Jesus turns six pots of water into wine at a wedding celebration in Cana of Galilee, which happens to be in the southern region of my home country of Lebanon. Would he not make a fantastic guest at any party? In John chapter 11, Jesus brings Lazarus back to life four days after his death, but have you ever heard of such a thing, aside from fictionalized zombie tales? There are countless stories to examine, but I suggest you read them all for yourselves, particularly Revelation, the final book of the New Testament, where you will find a troupe of bizarre creatures, including a dragon, terrifying angels, and a beast with seven heads and 666 on its body.

And certainly no discussion of Jesus' miracles can be complete without mention of His most notorious accomplishment—his reappearance three days after his

113

death. The resurrection of Jesus Christ has been interpreted by many as proof of his divinity, but no one in human history has actually experienced such an event, and it is nothing more than an imaginative piece of fiction. I guarantee that not one person alive today has seen or experienced anything remotely similar to the events described in any of these far-fetched stories, so why do people rely upon them as the foundation of their religious beliefs?

I see several reasons for this: the majority of believers have not actually read the books of their religions, or if they have, that they fear the consequences of questioning religious doctrine, the possibility of going to hell, or realizing that they have wrongly believed in God for all these years. Many cling to their views because they are ignorant of the current scientific knowledge of the natural world—if their religions claim to provide all the answers, why would they need to consider any other explanation, however valid it may be?

Moving beyond the bizarre occurrences and outlandish tales of the Old and New Testaments for a moment, let us now turn our attention to the portrayal of God's character in these books, as it appears to be neither merciful nor compassionate.

The Immorality of God

When asked to describe God's character, typical responses include loving, caring, forgiving, merciful, just, and moral. Believers usually ascribe to God the positive human attributes to which we all aspire; however, the Abrahamic God as depicted in the Bible and the Quran possess none of these qualities. The God of these books is vicious, cruel, vindictive, selfish, sexist, misogynistic, vengeful, immoral, jealous, hateful, an advocate for rape, and a blood-thirsty murderer.

Although I have evaluated God's character using these religious texts, I do not take them to be the Word of God, as I do not believe in the existence of supernatural deities. It is clear to me that these books were written thousands of years ago by men seeking to control other people through fear. Since most people have not read the actual texts upon which their religions are based, I believe that they do not know the true character of God and simply assign positive attributes to him. Many of those who have studied these books tend to focus on the positive aspects while ignoring the unpleasant ones because they are afraid to think poorly of a god who has the potential to punish them in this life and "the next."

God in the Old Testament

We begin with the early chapters of Genesis with the story of Adam and Eve, where Eve's creation from Adam's rib already positions men as the superior sex from the onset of humanity's existence. This status is reconfirmed when Adam blames Eve for eating the forbidden fruit, and later in Genesis 3:16 when God punishes her, like all women, with a life of suffering: "Great will be your pain in childbirth; in sorrow will your children come to birth; still your desire will be for your husband, but he will be your master." Does that sound like a forgiving, loving, and caring God, or a sexist, spiteful, and misogynistic one?

In the sixth chapter of Genesis, God decides to murder everyone on the planet because he views their behavior as sinful and corrupt, so he decides to flood the Earth, killing every living thing upon it except for Noah, his family, and the animals on the ark. If God were truly omnipotent, he would possess the power to come up with numerous solutions to the problem of humanity's sinful behavior. Instead, he destroys everything, but what does all other life on Earth have to do with the evil deeds of humankind? And even if we assume that killing is a justifiable punishment, why did he not spare innocent people and kill only the sinners? The only explanation for this seems to be that God is a cold-blooded murderer—regularly killing innocent people, babies, animals, and plants for no reason whatsoever.

In Genesis chapter 22, God orders Abraham to murder his own son in order to prove that he is both fearful of and loyal to God. Genesis 22:9-10 states: "Abraham went up to a mountain and made an altar and placed the wood on it, and having made tight the bands around Isaac, his son, he put him on the wood on the altar. And stretching out his hand, Abraham took the knife to put his son to death." Just as Abraham is about to kill his own child, an angel appears to stop him, since God is now able to confirm that Abraham indeed fears him. What a despicable story—can you imagine the fear and anguish that both Abraham and his son must have endured? Would you kill your child if God asked you to do so? Furthermore, would an all-knowing God not already be aware of whether or not Abraham feared him without this horrifying test; or did God put them through this ordeal simply to confirm a fact that he already knew? If you heard on the news that a man had murdered his son because "God told him to," how would you respond?

I have previously discussed the story of Moses and the Egyptian plagues, but I wish to reiterate that God simply used the Pharaoh to demonstrate His own power. God prevented the Pharaoh from permitting the Jews to leave Egypt so that he could purposefully inflict disease, pain, and suffering upon every single person and animal in the country. With the final plague, he kills every first born male in every family. He creates a problem and solution for which many innocent people suffer—are these the actions of a reasonable, compassionate, and just God?

In Exodus 21:2-6, God provides Moses with a series of laws in which He condones slavery by outlining numerous regulations regarding the subjugation and treatment of slaves: "If you get a Hebrew servant for money, he is to be your servant for six years, and in the seventh year you are to let him go free without payment...but if the servant says clearly, 'My master and my wife and children are dear to me; I have no desire to be free,' then his master...is to make a hole in his ear with a sharp-pointed instrument, and he will be his servant forever. If a man gives his man-servant or his woman-servant blows with a rod, causing death, he is certainly to undergo punishment. But, at the same time, if the servant goes on living for a day or two, the master is not to get punishment, for the servant is his property."

God specifically tells his people that slaves are their possessions and they are allowed to beat them—as long as the beating does not kill them in the next two days. If they die after three days, there is no consequence, but a slave dying within two days of a beating *does* warrant punishment. However, the master's penalty is not death, despite the fact that another of God's law states that if you kill someone then you should be put to death yourself. But I suppose in God's

118

sweet and gentle eyes, slaves do not count as humans. Personally, I am relieved that modern secular laws no longer follow God's orders, but in the past, they justified the common practice of slavery as well as many other horrible transgressions.

In Exodus 22:18 God tells His people: "Thou shall not suffer a witch to live." We all know there are no such things as witches, so imagine the millions of people, namely women, murdered because of this passage. In Exodus chapter 31, God states that if anyone works on the Sabbath, they should also be put to death, so keep in mind that if you work on Saturdays, the Bible states that you deserve to die. In the same chapter, God tells Moses to go to war with the Midianites and tells Moses to order the troops to kill everyone except the virgin girls, which they are allowed to keep for themselves. Can you imagine what these girls experienced, seeing their families massacred, not to mention being raped for the rest of their life by the "chosen people" of God?

In Exodus chapter 32, while Moses receives the Ten Commandments from God atop Mount Sinai, the People of Israel construct a golden ox to worship as their god and celebrate with a feast. Moses quickly descends the mountain at God's behest and tells His people in Exodus 32:26-27: "'Whoever is on the Lord's side, let him come to me,' and all the Levites gathered around him. He told them: 'This is

119

the word of the Lord, the God of Israel. Let every man take his sword at his side, and go from one end of the tents to the other, killing his brother and his friend and his neighbor.'" The men did as Moses instructed, and killed approximately 3,000 people that day. Does a merciful and decent God order people to murder their friends and family members? '

In Leviticus chapter 15, God provides guidelines for the treatment of women on their menstrual cycle. I suggest you read the entire chapter for yourself to see how absurd and degrading these rules are, but here is one example from Leviticus 15:19-21: "If a woman has a flow of blood from her body, she will have to be kept separate for seven days, and anyone touching her will be unclean till evening. And anyone touching anything on which she has been seated will have to have his clothing washed and his body bathed in water and be unclean till evening."

In Leviticus 20, God delivers His laws concerning sexual matters to His people, and verses 10-14 are particularly severe: "If a man has sex relations with another man's wife, even the wife of his neighbor, he and she are certainly to be put to death. The man who has sex relations with his father's wife has put shame on his father: the two of them are to be put to death. If a man has sex relations with his son's wife, the two of them are to be put to death. If a man has sex relations with a man, the two of them have done a disgusting thing: let them be put to death. If a man takes as

120

wife a woman and her mother, it is an act of shame; let them be burned with fire, all three of them."

As made clear by the previous examples, murder seems to be the solution to all of God's perceived problems with human sexuality. Coincidentally, there is no mention in the Bible of two women having sex with each other, so it must be considered acceptable—do you think this has anything to do with the fact that this book was written by men? Furthermore, did any of these guidelines apply when God created Adam and Eve, and they were the only two people on the planet, or when Lot and his two daughters were left in a desolate cave? Some, if not all of these rules must have been broken, especially considering the fact that it would be entirely counterproductive, since according to Leviticus chapter 20, committing incest is punishable by death. However, God does seem to condone it in certain circumstances.

In Leviticus 21:16-21, God informs us that he hates the disabled: "And the Lord said to Moses, say to Aaron, 'If a man of your family, in any generation, is damaged in body, let him not come near to make the offering of the bread of his God; for any man whose body is damaged may not come near: one who is blind, or has not the use of his legs, or one who has a broken nose or any unnatural growth, or a man with broken feet or hands, or one whose back is bent, or one who is unnaturally small, or one who has a damaged eye, or whose skin is diseased, or whose sex parts are damaged; no man of the offspring of Aaron whose body is damaged in any way may come near to give the fire offerings of the Lord; he is damaged.'"

In Leviticus 26:27-29, God instructs his followers on what to do with people who speak against him: "But if you do not give ear to Me, and do not keep all these my laws, and if you go against My rules and if you have hate in your souls for My decisions, and you do not do all My orders but go against my agreement, then My wrath will be burning against you, and I will give you punishment, I myself, seven times for your sins. Then you will take the flesh of your sons and the flesh of your daughters for food." Is this a loving and compassionate God, or a repulsive, vengeful monster?

In Numbers chapter 16, God murders 14,700 people by plaguing them with disease, burning others to death, and even opening the Earth so that additional sinners may fall into the underworld. In Numbers 21:6 God sends poisonous snakes to kill some of His own people who spoke against him, and in Numbers chapter 25, he murders another 24,000 of His devotees with an infectious disease. As surprising as it is to find God punishing his own supporters this severely, Deuteronomy 19:21 shows God encouraging his followers to also show a similar callousness to their enemies: "Have no pity; let life be given for life, eye for eye, tooth for tooth, hand for hand, foot for foot." In Deuteronomy 28, God explains more consequences of not obeying his laws, and it is one of the most hateful chapters in the Old Testament. You must read it for yourself to fully understand how effectively it terrifies people into solemn obedience to God.

Numerous chapters throughout the Bible, particularly chapter 22 of Deuteronomy, reveal God's misogynistic and sexist nature. Verse 21 states that if a husband discovers that his wife was not a virgin at the time of their marriage, then: "They are to make the girl come to the door of her father's house and she will be stoned to death by the men of the town, because she has done evil and put shame on Israel, by acting as a loose woman in her father's house." In Leviticus 21:9, God states that we should gruesomely murder certain women for having multiple sexual partners: "If the daughter of a priest makes herself common and by her loose behavior puts shame on her father, let her be burned with fire."

As sinister as the previous verses were, I am particularly disgusted by this law from Deuteronomy 22:28-29: "If a man sees a young virgin, who has not given her word to be married to anyone, and he takes her by force and has connection with her, and discovery is made of it, then the man will have to give the virgin's father 50 shekels of silver and make her his wife because he has put shame on her."

In addition to the horrible crime already committed against her, the woman is further punished for the rest of her life by having to live with the man who forced himself on her—I find the moral message in this law completely appalling. Can you imagine enduring the most horrifying moment that any woman dreads, especially as a virgin, and then being required to live with your attacker, repeatedly subjected to rape? In addition, this law allows—and even encourages—any monster with 50 shekels of silver to choose a virgin girl he wants to marry and then rape her. I cannot express my anger at the ignorance of people choosing to believe in the imagined virtues of this God rather than reading the tangible document detailing his repulsive wishes and desires. I am furious to think that for thousands of years, this God rewarded these dreadful brutes who belonged in prisons or graves. This is but one of many indications that this "holy book" was written by highly immoral men for their own benefit.

This horrific story from Judges 11:29-31 further exemplifies God's misogynistic behavior: "Then the spirit of the Lord came on Jephthah, and he went through Gilead and Manasseh, and came to Mize of Gilead…and Jephthah took an oath to the Lord and said, 'If you will give the children of Ammon into my hands, then whoever comes out from the door of my house, meeting me when I come back in peace from the children of Ammon, will be the Lord's and I will give him as a burned offering.'" Jephthah does win the war and who should greet him upon returning home, but his

124

virgin daughter? Jephthah informs her that he had promised God that he would burn her to death. The daughter somehow understands this twisted logic, and simply asks her father to give her two months to spend with her friends before he kills her. He agrees, and then burns her alive in the name of God once the two months transpires. At no point during that time did God suggest otherwise, so he obviously wished for this horrendous event to occur. Do you recall the story of Abraham and his son Isaac, wherein God stopped Abraham from murdering his son at the last possible moment? Clearly, he could have done the same in this situation, but preferred to have the burnt offering of a young virgin. I have no explanation for this, other than that the God of the Bible is completely perverse and misogynistic.

In 2 Samuel chapters 11-12, King David impregnates another man's wife and sends her husband to die in a war to divert attention from the affair. David then marries this woman, but God kills their child as punishment because he is unhappy with David. David's wife later gives birth to another son, by which time David has straightened up his act, so God leaves this child alone. Did God not previously introduce a different punishment for adultery? Leviticus 20:10 immediately comes to mind: "And if a man has sex relations with another man's wife, even the wife of his neighbor, he and she are certainly to be put to death." However, in this case, God decides that the best solution would not be to punish the sinners who disobeyed his rules, but to kill two innocent victims instead—a baby and an unwitting husband. Although such a law would not surprise me, nowhere in my study of the Old Testament did I come across a decree that if a man sleeps with another man's wife, her husband is to be killed, along with the child resulting from the adulterous act.

In 2 Samuel 24:12, King David goes against God's orders and God sends him a message: "Three things are offered to you: say which of them you will have, and I will do it to you...are there to be three years when there is not enough food in your land? Or will you go in flight from your haters for three months while they go after you? Or will you have three days of violent disease in your land? Take thought and say what answer I am to give to Him who sent me."

King David chooses three days of disease for his subjects, which results in God killing 70,000 people. Why must so many innocent lives be lost for one person's mistake, while that person is spared entirely? What kind of twisted justice does God offer by allowing a king to cowardly pass his sentence on to his people? The Old Testament verses provide countless examples of God's immoral behavior, and I now wish to take a slightly different approach to our continued examination of the true character of God as shown by his actions in the New Testament.

God in the New Testament

I will not spend time analyzing verses from the New Testament, but will instead provide a brief summary of God's depravity. I would like to mention that many Christians attempt to disassociate themselves from the abominations of the Old Testament, arguing that Jesus came to show them a new and better way, but they cannot disregard the first half of this holy book without also dismissing their creation story, the concept of original sin, and the first prophets who received God's commandments: Abraham, Noah, and Moses.

In several verses of the Bible, Jesus specifically states that not only are the laws of the Old Testament valid, but that he has also come to uphold them, first in 2 Timothy 3:16: "All Scripture is inspired by God and is useful to teach us what is true and to make us realize what is wrong in our lives," and later in Matthew 5:17: "Do not think that I have come to abolish the Law or the Prophets; I have not come to abolish them but to fulfill them."

Though God endowed us with the concept of original sin, he also orchestrated the punishment, torture, and human sacrifice of Jesus Christ as a way for humanity to be rescued from eternal damnation and suffering. The catch is that each individual must accept Jesus as their savior in order to be forgiven and avoid this torturous fate, and the Bible is quite clear that anyone who does not will be sent to hell.

Listen to what gentle and loving Jesus says in Luke 19:27 about the fate of non-believers: "And as for those who were against me, who would not have Me for their ruler, let them come here and be put to death before Me." It seems that God prematurely condemns humanity to a terrible fate, then offers a single avenue of escape contingent on perpetual devotion to his son.

In addition to the introduction of hell in the New Testament, Jesus establishes the notion of "thought crime" in Matthew 5:27-28, where people can now be judged and punished even for their thoughts: "You have knowledge that it was said, 'You may not have connection with another man's wife.' But I say to you that everyone whose eyes are turned on a woman with desire has had connection with her in his heart." This example is just one of many fear tactics employed by various religious groups—believers are discouraged from questioning or contemplating any ideas that may oppose their religious dogma due to fear of repercussions.

I understand this thought process intimately because I also used to dismiss any and all ideas that opposed my religious beliefs as quickly as I could, fearing that God could surely hear them and know that I had been pondering His existence. I cured myself of this intellectual disease by learning to think critically and gaining the courage to ask difficult questions about my beliefs instead of immediately chasing any contradictory ideas out of my mind for fear of incurring God's wrath. The Bible threatens sinners and non-believers with frightening imagery of an eternity spent in misery, torment, and torture in hell. Anyone who does not declare Jesus Christ their personal savior can look forward to a sulfurous lake of fire in hell surrounded by horrible beasts gnashing their teeth. Fear of punishment by God, and in particular the threat of spending eternity in hell, prevents many people from honestly examining some of the implausible aspects of their own religious doctrines, but the threat of an imaginary punishment should not stand in the way of thinking logically. I encourage you to take an unflinching look at some of these outlandish passages and truly consider the nature of God as depicted in these texts.

In my opinion, the underlying concepts of the New Testament are enough to effectively illustrate the true behavior of the Abrahamic God: depraved, vicious, and controlling. As previously mentioned, I feel that I am unable to speak directly about the Quran, but I will say that the God of the Quran is the same God that is depicted in the Old and New Testaments of the Christian Bible. Additionally, the Quran emphasizes the threat of punishment in hell ten-fold and describes it in much greater detail. If you truly examine these books, you will acknowledge that God's cruel actions vastly supersede any wrongdoing by the devil. I invite you to seriously contemplate the idea that according to the Bible itself, the devil appears much kinder, and in fact, less evil than God.

Fear of Asking Questions

One of the most basic attributes of human behavior is our inquisitive nature, yet religions discourage this characteristic by forcing us to believe in "the Word of God" as told by his messengers. We are unknowingly robbed of this unique virtue and left to passively ingest this message without giving ourselves the chance to actively investigate the answers to life's important questions. Religions blind us to the fact that we are a part of the natural world and force us to accept a rigid doctrine as truth, or else face the threat of a terrible afterlife full of horrible punishments. Along with questioning the validity of its tenets, religious leaders often discourage believers from comparing their faith to others in an attempt to determine which is the 'right' one.

It is crucial to emphasize that I do not blame any individual for holding onto these beliefs, as I once did myself. When I look back on the way I used to think, I knew nothing of the natural world—the universe, Earth, other planets, the moon, the sun, or the stars. I did not need to wonder about these things because I believed that God had constructed the universe and placed me—along with everything else that he created—on Earth. Since this false truth had been drilled into me from birth, I did not care about anything else in existence. Like many others, fear of punishment in the afterlife prevented me from exploring other possibilities, but when I lost my belief in God, I came to realize that the relationship I once had with him was actually between myself and a figment of my imagination. Since that relationship was the only thing I valued, I then realized that I was only caring about myself. I saw that the toxicity of religious belief took away so much of my human nature and replaced it with an imaginary man in my head, which in reality, was really simply a part of my own inner monologue.

It must be emphasized that many deeply-rooted pathological complications stem from a permanently fixed belief in God's omnipotence—that he controls everything and is capable of anything. Therefore, most believers tend to leave the world's troubles—global warming, destruction of nature, war, suffering, injustice, and misery—in the hands of God. These individuals ask God to fix these problems, as though this act has any effect on the world. This detrimental way of thinking also leeches into our everyday lives, where praying for God to save you from your troubles actually prevents you from finding real solutions. This skewed psychological system of a belief in God detaches us from our true natural origins, giving us the false premise that we are made in God's image, superior to nature and other creatures.

At the same time, this mindset eliminates the sense of personal responsibility for the world's problems and the suffering of our fellow human beings.

I personally grew up in a religious environment where everyday phrases such as "If God wills it, it will be so;" "Only God knows why;" and "May God help them," perfectly illustrate this attitude, and such expressions often escaped my lips during my time as a believer. By uttering these phrases in those moments rather than taking action, I was simply mitigating a problem by leaving it for God to deal with, while I conveniently forgot the issue and moved on with my life. The gravely twisted aspect of this situation is that while I prayed for God to help friends or the poor, I actually felt pleased with myself for doing so and that I was part of the solution. This way of thinking takes place daily in the mind of a believer, relieving the individual from accepting responsibility and taking steps toward real solutions, and herein lies the inherent selfishness of holding a rigid belief in God as an omnipotent being. We must step back to examine this toxic belief and realize that transferring responsibility to God—whose existence or intervention on our behalf has never been proven—actually removes us from reality. It is time to see that we are the ones who must stand up to remedy the wrongs of the world as well as the problems in our own lives.

Though my own way of thinking had also been programmed in this irregular manner, I eventually dared to escape this trap and began to examine the world around me. I found that there have been thousands of gods and multitudes of religions throughout mankind's history. I then asked myself: if God truly does exist, why would he have had us believe in so many different forms of him throughout human history and allow us to continually kill one another to prove that our particular version of him is the correct one? I now believe that religion is a system of destruction—to the self as well as humanity at large. Because I no longer feared God's punishment, I was able to truly and openly examine the actions of the leaders of religious groups. By realizing how much death and destruction they have brought to this world, I came to see the absurdity of religious doctrines. I found I could no longer believe in the "miracles" that had no proof of ever occurring, and based on scientific laws and principles, could not have ever transpired.

There is no proof whatsoever with which to investigate or even consider the existence of a supernatural realm. Instead, all mention of such occurrences point to fabricated stories in books written thousands of years ago, at a time where our scientific knowledge was rudimentary at best. I openly challenge anyone to present evidence that the supernatural stories found in any religious text actually occurred. However, I remain confident this task is impossible because it is common knowledge that snakes do not talk, a sea will not split because someone commands it to do so, one person cannot kill a thousand men with the jawbone of a donkey, virgin births are impossible, water cannot be turned into wine, no one can walk on water, and certainly no one can die and come back to life after three days.

Faith

For the majority of believers, the idea of eternal devotion replaces the need to ask questions. Religious people often say that they have faith that God exists, but this word is simply an assurance for individuals who have no concrete evidence of their beliefs. If there was proof of God's existence, it would surely be presented, but it seems as though the concept of faith is a convenient solution to this problem. In the last 10,000 years, there have been roughly 10,000 religions that worshipped an estimated 1,000 gods, and as such, the religion and concept of God (or gods) one believes in is contingent upon both geography and time. The believers of the past and present religions certainly had/have faith that their God or gods exist, but how can everyone be correct?

I will note that faith does tend to have positive connotations in our society, despite the fact that it means believing in something without any supporting proof. However, conviction without evidence is a dangerous and detrimental human ideology, and has caused the destruction of both our minds and our environment. Faith is nearly always irrational because it cannot be investigated or measured.

Many people tend to cling to these false constructs rather than view the world objectively due to a cerebral process that cognitive psychology refers to as the confirmation bias—the tendency to only accept and process information that validates our beliefs, while ignoring all other information that contradicts those ideals, no matter how reliable or factual this new evidence may be. When people think their beliefs are the absolute truth, no matter what anyone else says or concrete evidence disputes, they place themselves in a state of ignorance that prevents them from learning anything new. Our ideas and beliefs ought to remain open to revision and we should not view being wrong in a negative light, but rather as an opportunity to expand our knowledge and grow. Examining your own religious beliefs with a bit of critical thinking will free you from the trap of hypocrisy that many believers fall into. For example, if you truly believe that this life is a test to demonstrate your worthiness of advancing to heaven, should you not spend every moment trying to earn that place through good deeds, or giving away your worldly possessions, as the Bible dictates? Should your only objective in life not be to follow the laws of God from the Bible in order to avoid an eternity of punishment in hell?

Prayer and the Soul Invention

Religious followers continue to believe that prayer influences reality, yet many studies have determined that prayer has no real effect other than simply providing comfort for the person who is praying. One famous study by a Christian organization in the United States, the John Templeton Foundation, investigated God's ability to directly intervene on a patient's behalf as a result of prayer. The study involved 1,800 patients undergoing heart bypass surgery. The patients were divided into two groups, one of which received prayers and another did not. None of the patients were told which group they belonged to, but in a third control group, the patients were told that they were being prayed for. The Templeton Foundation spent 2.4 million of their own dollars on this study, along with 2.3 million from the US federal government, but the results of the study, published in 2006, did little to support the argument that prayer improves the outcome of any given situation. For example, 59% of people in the control group (who knew they were being prayed for) suffered more complications than those in the groups who did not know

136

they were being prayed for. Another 18% of those in the group who did not know they were being prayed for suffered major complications (including heart attacks) compared to only 13% in the group that did not receive prayers at all. Not even a 4.7-million-dollar study of 1,800 patients and the eyes of the entire world were enough for God to prove that He listens to or responds to prayers.

Granted, praying does have several benefits, since it relieves stress and provides a sense of comfort, but who are we actually praying to, other than a glorified version of ourselves? Studies in the fields of psychology have demonstrated that within your mind, you are not simply one person, but one of many different characters depending on a variety of situations. When a person perceives the idea of God, psychologically-speaking, they are simply creating yet another of these characters. Since prayers do not exist in the physical reality, the act of praying is simply talking to yourself, and though it can offer the individual a sense of well-being, it has absolutely no effect on the outside world.

Much like the idea of prayer, the concept of a soul has also been directly attributed to religious beliefs, but these constructs are nothing more than fabrications. Consciousness cannot exist independently from the brain; when our brain dies, our consciousness dies along with it. We can observe neurons firing when someone has a thought, making who we think we are nothing more than a collection of physiological processes. Everything we experience is a construct of this physical brain, and when it dies, our mind ceases to exist.

Suffering and the Afterlife

We evolved as biological creatures on the plains of Africa, programmed to survive various extreme conditions. Evolution did not shape us into perfect machines; it only created organisms that were better equipped to function with the surrounding resources. Perhaps the belief in an idyllic afterlife consoled us and helped us cope with our harsh reality; a rare example of religious beliefs providing an evolutionary benefit rather than detriment to our specie's survival.

The human mind developed the concept of an afterlife because our consciousness evolved the intelligence to comprehend the unfortunate fact that we will eventually die. The creation of the afterlife is simply a reaction, or biological byproduct, of our advanced consciousness attempting to comprehend this new and disturbing notion. We find no concrete evidence of such a concept, but scientific studies demonstrate that being alive is purely a biological process, the sum of metabolic chemistry in our bodies and brain. When these mechanisms stop functioning, the 'us' in our bodies ceases to exist.

I no longer feel the need to hope for an afterlife, because I have come to feel completely happy to be alive in the present one. We all wish to make sense of our experience on Earth, but the search for these answers can leave us feeling hollow or unfulfilled. In many societies, this emptiness is occupied with the false idea of God, but since we inherently seek awareness and understanding of ourselves and our environment, the void within us ought to be filled by the pursuit of knowledge, as well as personal and collective growth. I believe that the only way we can truly live beyond this earthly experience is by leaving something behind for people to remember us by, whether it be a book, a work of art, a scientific discovery, new technology, or simply our kind actions.

Science vs Religion

In order to find a way to reconcile our current scientific knowledge of reality with the supernatural, many devout believers today assert that God exists outside the universe and the natural world, but this is yet another assertion with no proof whatsoever. If we accept the idea that God exists outside the universe, how is he then able to intervene and affect the outcome of events on Earth? If he were to interfere with reality, we would be able to empirically test these "miracles," which would defy the natural laws of physics. If he did not interfere with reality, there is no way to experience his presence, and the universe would look and function the same whether it was created by God or created as the result of the Big Bang.

One point that must be emphasized here is that the vast majority of our scientific knowledge was acquired relatively recently. For hundreds of thousands of years, we lived in ignorance of the natural world and adopted false beliefs of how we came to be and how the world around us functioned. It was not until the last several hundred years that humans were able to develop the medical and technological advances which helped us paint a more accurate picture of our earthly and celestial surroundings, based on scientific fact and the physical laws of nature.

Scientific inquiry requires proof, while religion relies upon a lack of evidence, often referred to as "faith." Science investigates what exists concretely, yet religion advocates simply hoping that God and heaven exist, with no proof based in objective reality. Science encourages skeptical inquiry and relies on evidence that is continually checked and rechecked. Religion forces us to believe in an ultimate truth that does not exist to begin with. Science is observable, repeatable, and empirical, while the tales of the Bible and alleged miracles are the opposite. Science is all about open and honest investigation—unlike religion, there are no authorities, and the investigatory process of peer

140

review is welcomed. Without a doubt, the scientific method is the most consistent, reliable, and self-correcting tool we possess to separate the truth from falsehood in our objective reality. The path to scientific knowledge which allowed us to understand how we are interconnected to the universe and all life on this planet is an amazingly beautiful narrative, much more inspiring than the peculiar creation stories presented by religious doctrines.

CHAPTER FIVE

THE SYSTEM

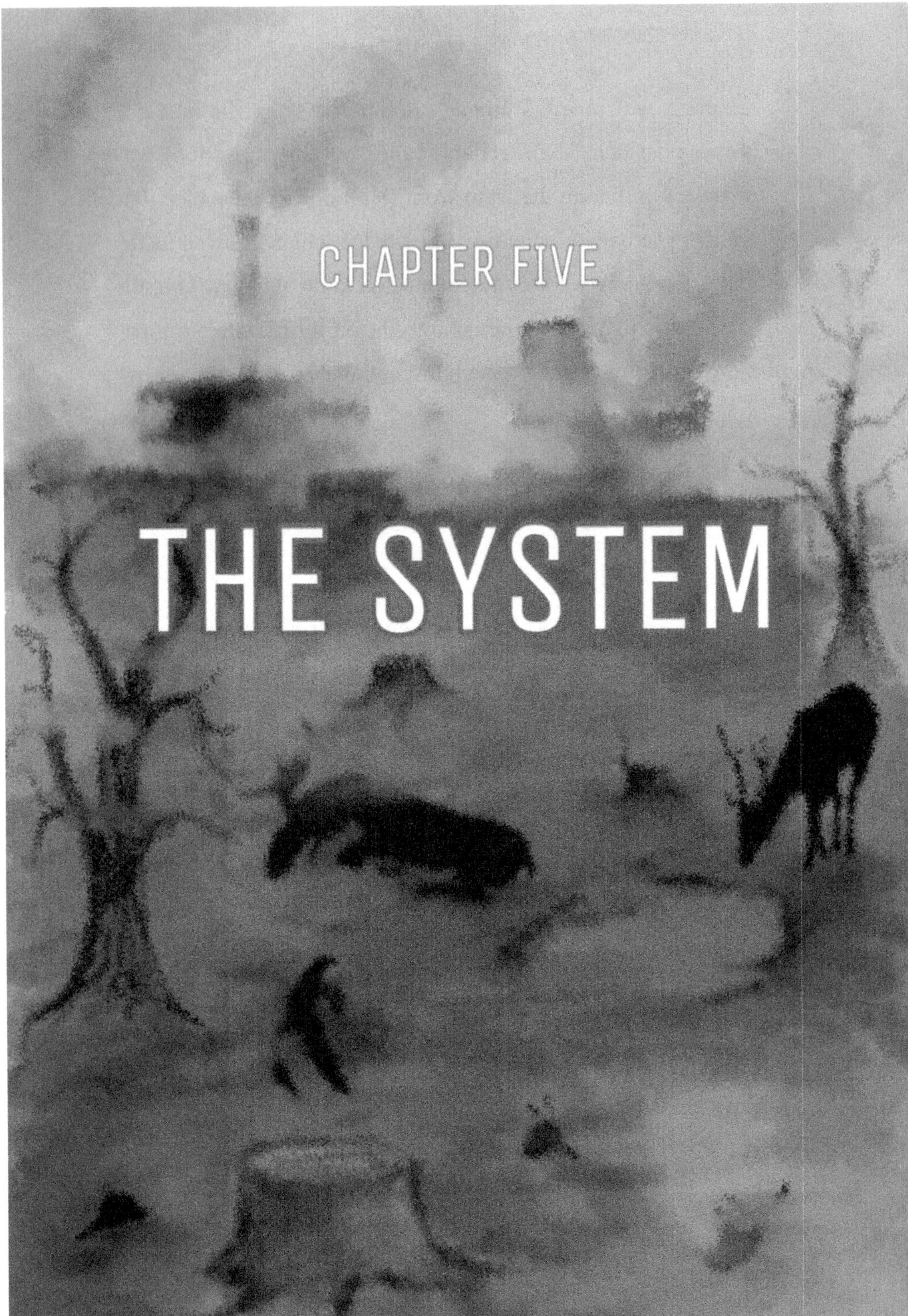

The System

Welcome to the system—money, greed, competition, selfishness, possessions, materialism, poverty, famine, war, pollution, global warming, and the destruction of nature. Immerse yourself in the imaginary and meaningless world of television, social media, advertisements, news, misinformation, judgment, confusion, and alienation. Unfortunately, we are all born into this system and therefore directly contribute to the negative outcomes it produces. For the majority of us, two institutions control our lives: religion and the monetary system. Religion offers us a false narrative of the reasons for our existence, and the monetary system provides us with the incorrect notion that our purpose in life amounts to simply earning money. A substantial portion of our income goes toward purchasing increasingly "improved" products that we are made to believe will increase our happiness and sense of well-being.

In order to produce a brainwashed human controlled by religious institutions, banks, militaries, and corporations, we are taught from a very young age that we must achieve a certain image to gain importance within this system. Unfortunately, attaining status in the society we live in often comes from the negative characteristics of humanity— aggression, competition, selfishness, and egotism—resulting in war, conflicts, hatred, and especially the oppression of the weak and impoverished. Along with the media and education system, this creates a monstrously detrimental mechanism that shapes and controls our behavior. Run by profit-seeking corporations, this structure perpetuates a cycle of pollution, starvation, depravation, and debt where human lives and the environment are of little concern to those at the helm of this twisted configuration.

Corporations and Wealth

In many cases, corporations have surpassed government institutions to become the most powerful organizations ever created. With financial gain as its primary goal, a corporation consumes resources in order to generate as much revenue as possible for its investors, regardless of human rights or environmental law violations. These influential entities control the majority of the world's resources and supplies, including food, water, medication, oil, infrastructure, and technology.

Although we possess the expertise and equipment to sustainably produce durable merchandise, it does not yield as great a profit for these corporations, which often spend more on advertising and conditioning the public to buy their products than on manufacturing quality merchandise. As very few goods are built to last, "new and improved" products fill the shelves every six months or so, with our planet taking the greatest hit. As more and more materials are consumed to create these new products, electronics, plastic, and toxic trash pile up all over the world.

As of 2019, a substantial portion of the $360 trillion worth of wealth in the world remains concentrated in North America, Australia, and Europe. The majority of this fortune was created in the early 1800s by relying upon a structure of debt which enslaved a large percentage of the world's population. Those living in impoverished regions suffer every day as a result of this monetary system supported by wealthy Western nations, their armies, and corporations. If a developing country wishes to provide infrastructure for its people, wealthier countries will offer loans from the World Bank or the International Monetary Fund (IMF). These loans finance infrastructure such as power plants, industrial parks, and ports, which often directly benefit the corporations that built them instead of the citizens of these countries. Once these countries are in debt and unable to repay the loans, the real robbery begins. The corporations send in "economic hitmen" to strike deals with the leaders of the impoverished nations by advising them to sell their resources cheaply, support them in the next war, and so on. If the leaders of these countries refuse the demands of the corporations, they are assassinated or overthrown for trying to return justice, equality, and freedom to their people. As seen in the cases of Guatemala, Panama, Vietnam, Ecuador, Chile, Venezuela,

Iran, and Iraq, wealthy nations—and the United States in particular—are unafraid to use military force when other strategies fail.

As long as this economic machine rules the world, wars, poverty, suffering, and distrust are guaranteed to be a part of our lives, but the bottom line is that we do need *some* sort of money to acquire food, water, and shelter to survive. If you can make just enough to do so, you are less of a slave to this system, and if you can manage to not make any money at all, then you are completely liberated from it. I believe that the less money and fewer possessions one owns, the freer one is, since no obligations hold them down. You must find your freedom by reconnecting yourself to humanity, life on Earth, and the universe, rather than serving as a cog in this destructive financial mechanism which has become the primary source of ignorance, misery, negativity, and suffering—both mentally and physically—in our world.

Poverty and the Education System

It is quite clear that under this economic structure, the rich are growing richer while the poor become further impoverished. The IMF and the World Bank have been assigned the task of imposing structural adjustment packages on the poor and developing nations, often forcing them to privatize their resource or industries in order to pay off their

146

impossible loan balances. The countries are robbed of their natural wealth, yet must continue to make payments as they plunge deeper and deeper into a debt structure that represents a form of modern-day colonialism.

Attaining wealth is highly valued within our destructive society, and therein lies the main problem. We mistakenly judge others on how much they own as a measure of virtue, yet often overlook the fact that in order for a small percentage to attain such wealth, a larger percentage must be enslaved. Additionally, I believe that the preservation and protection of this imbalanced financial system is perpetuated by the formal education we are all subjected to.

The public education system began in the 19th century as a product of industrialization, with individual human beings molded to serve the purpose of manufacturing conglomerates. Even today, the education system often predicates the field of work one enters—if you wish to pursue a vocation in the arts, you will likely be discouraged on the basis that you will not earn much money. People also tend to believe that holding multiple college degrees proves one's intelligence, but this simply demonstrates an ability to pay for the degree, it does not guarantee employment or success, as evidenced by the large percentage of students who obtain their college degrees at a high personal cost, only to return home jobless and thousands of dollars in debt.

Today's education system aims to produce productive, robotic drones who earn money for the corporate world, instead of developing the unique attributes of each student. Once they are employed, the goals that workers are forced to serve do not hold any personal value, but unfortunately we are conditioned to be integrated into the profit-earning system from a young age. Intelligence is diverse, distinct, and dynamic; yet these attributes are regularly discouraged in our education system, which focuses solely on increasing profits, creating a dangerous potential for the destruction of our natural world due to misappropriation of technological advancements.

The Misuse of Technology

Technology has greatly enhanced our lives and helped make us the species we are today. Our homes, cars, running water, electricity and even clothes are the result of scientific exploration and technological development. These modern conveniences would not be possible if we simply placed our confidence in religious, financial, or political institutions; however, our dependence upon natural resources to provide these amenities has increasingly tied us to this negative system that harms our planet and threatens the very survival of our species.

We already possess the necessary technologies to eliminate our dependence on fossil fuel, which is the main cause of global warming. However, the heads of fossil fuel corporations do not allow renewable energy technologies to be available to the public. There is enough solar, wind, tidal, and geothermal energy to power the world's infrastructures forever, but if those resources are freely given by nature, corporations can no longer profit. Though technology has improved our daily lives, its systematic misuse is leading to the destruction of nature and the demise of our species.

Global Warming

The Earth's atmosphere is composed of a mixture of carbon dioxide (CO_2), methane (CH_4), ozone (O_3), and nitrous oxide (N_2O). A precise balance of these greenhouse gases is critical for life on our planet to exist, and an excess or diminished amount of any one of them could lead to a global warming or cooling event, such as the ice age that occurred roughly 18,000 years ago. During that time, the global temperature was 5 °C cooler than it currently is due to a lack of greenhouse gases in our atmosphere.

Since the industrial revolution took off roughly 260 years ago, we have been burning fuel and coal at an extremely rapid rate, releasing huge amounts of carbon dioxide into the atmosphere. Methane, released as a byproduct of cattle domestication, is also to blame, as it is 30 times more potent than CO_2. Our transportation methods also greatly contribute to global warming: up to 15% of greenhouse emissions come from automobiles, and our increasing use of appliances and gadgets make us further reliant upon the energy grid. Coal, oil, and natural gas account for 90% of the world's energy resources, and burning them continually increases the buildup of CO_2 in the atmosphere.

Global warming translates to a small rise in the Earth's temperature, which increases the number of super storms, heat waves, droughts, and floods around the world. As the global temperature surges, polar ice begins to melt, creating a continuous cycle of temperature escalation. Polar ice keeps Earth's temperature cooler by reflecting sunlight and heat from its surface, while water traps the sun's heat, causing the global temperature to rise. If the global temperature rose by even two or three degrees Celsius, we could reach a tipping point where Arctic ice is unable to form, resulting in a cycle of ever-increasing temperatures and catastrophic weather. This may not seem like a significant amount, but the Earth's temperature is one degree Celsius warmer than it has been for the last thousands of years, and even a five-degree fluctuation could completely wipe our species from the planet. Geological events such as erupting supervolcanoes and astronomical impacts have caused extreme global warming on many occasions throughout the Earth's history, and caused mass extinctions resulting in the disappearance of 75-90% of life on the planet. However, many of us have seen rapid climate change even within our own lifetime, and the blame for this alarming phenomenon falls squarely upon our shoulders.

There is no debating the fact that our planet's temperature is on the rise—thousands of research vessels in the sea and tens of thousands of climate observatories along with more than a hundred satellites orbit our planet, providing feedback to teams of Nobel Prize-winning researchers using supercomputers to analyze this data. These scientists have created extensive models of past weather patterns as well as approximations of future ones. Based on this research, if we continue pumping greenhouse gases into the atmosphere at our current rate, by the second half of this century, the global temperature could surge up to 3 °C. This can cause the glaciers in the Himalayas to disappear, leaving billions in the area without water. The melting of the Greenland ice sheet may become irreversible, causing sea levels to rise drastically around the world. The Amazon Rainforest—known as "the lungs of the Earth" since it absorbs huge amounts of carbon dioxide and produces 20% of the world's oxygen—could completely disappear. Massive fires in this incredible forest would release so much CO_2 that the global temperature would increase by at least another degree, further exacerbating the cycle of global warming. The Amazon Rainforest would be permanently lost and leave an abundance of CO_2 in the air, which would only continue to steadily increase the planet's temperature.

If we continue burning fossil fuels at our current rate and destroying the very nature we depend on, our species will surely disappear. Evidence of our presence on this planet would quickly be erased—dust and vegetation would blanket our cities, and life would continue as though we had never existed. By the end of our wasteful journey on Earth, humanity would have wiped out countless species and would be just another failed experiment in the story of life on this planet. And who knows, perhaps other creatures more deserving of a higher consciousness would later attain it; if they are smarter and more adaptable than ourselves, they will discover and learn from the way we caused the destruction of our own species, and be able to live in peace and harmony together.

Water is Not for Sale

The presence of water on Earth was the crucial element that led to the formation of life on this planet. Since the first signs of life appeared approximately 3.8 billion years ago, every organism has depended on water for its survival, yet we are the only species to threaten every living organism on Earth—including our own—by exploiting this priceless resource. As our population approaches 7.8 billion, water has become increasingly scarce, and an estimated one billion people around the world do not have access to clean water. This results in the death of approximately 3.4 million people per year, including 6,000 children every day, often due to waterborne diseases. One cause of this crisis is the infiltration of corporations into developing countries, and the privatization of fresh water supplies in exchange for debt reduction programs. By shifting from public to private ownership, the government surrenders its power to corporations, leaving its people at the mercy of business-minded machines. Since the main goal of a private business is profit maximization, increased water prices ensue, and the poor are forced to seek alternative water sources; in many cases, ones that have been contaminated by human activity.

Because water exists in one of three states: liquid, ice, or vapor, the Earth's water supply is continually recycled between the ground and the air. During this natural exchange—known as the hydrologic cycle—water is neither gained nor lost, but simply changes forms as it travels. When the water supply in a certain region becomes privatized, a corporation will often dam a river or install pumps to retrieve underground water stores called aquifers. Both of these methods interrupt the natural hydrologic cycle, leading to the degradation of the surrounding environment, as well as the water quality.

Modern technological advancements now facilitate the pumping of massive amounts of water from underground aquifers. When water is transported away from the land it originated from, the water source is depleted faster than it can naturally replenish itself, which leads to geological destruction in the immediate area, as well as desertification of the surrounding areas. Once water near an aquifer has been depleted for agricultural purposes, it seeps back into the ground, altered by the chemical products of commercial farming. As the cycle repeats itself, the water becomes increasingly polluted with fertilizers and pesticides until the entire reserve becomes contaminated.

Dams also adversely affect the hydrologic cycle in a variety of ways. The majority of these man-made attempts to control the natural flow of water are privately owned, built by corporations to produce hydroelectricity or to divert water for agricultural use. A dam significantly changes the ecology of a river by reducing the amount of water available downstream, often causing the surrounding wetlands to dry up. However, these wetlands are a crucial part of a natural cleansing process for the water, trapping and filtering pollutants as water passes through the hydrologic cycle. In fact, dams built in the last 100 years have destroyed more than 60% of wetlands around the world. Furthermore, when free-flowing water is hindered, the organic material, essential nutrients, and minerals that sustain ecosystems along the river become trapped. This eventually renders the still water behind the dam completely unusable: as the organic material begins to decay, it releases methane gas, not only polluting the surrounding land, but contributing to the greenhouse effect. It is estimated that the effects of a dam on global warming could be 10 times more harmful than that of a coal plant.

Another way the privatization of water degrades our environment is the manufacture of disposable plastic water bottles by corporations. The main ingredient in plastic bottles is polyethylene terephthalate, or PET. PET is manufactured in petrochemical plants, releasing a trail of toxic byproducts into the environment.

The alarming consequences of manufacturing plastic water bottles are only half the issue—the other half is their disposal. For example, the United States consumes 80 million plastic water bottles daily, yet only 20% of those bottles are recycled. The remaining 80% are dumped in landfills, and when it rains, these buoyant vessels make their way into streams, rivers, and oceans. In the Pacific Ocean, there is an accumulation of trash known as the Eastern Garbage Patch, which is twice the size of Texas. Similar garbage patches have been discovered in the North and South Atlantic, the South Pacific, and the Indian Oceans. In

1999, a survey was conducted on the Eastern Garbage Patch which revealed it contained six times more plastic than plankton, and a similar survey of the same area in 2008 calculated 46 times more plastic than plankton.

A United Nations conference in 1992 declared water an economic good, a decision that transformed it from a life-giving source which ought to be free and readily available to all into a corporate-controlled commodity with a value based on supply and demand. This concept turned the distribution and sale of water into a nearly $700 billion global industry.

In African countries where the water supply has been privatized, the price of drinking water has risen so greatly that only the wealthiest can afford it. In the poorer rural areas, private corporations severely limit access to community faucets, often going so far as to install electric meters on them. The underprivileged (which constitute a great majority of Africa's population) are unable to afford the high prices, and are forced to seek contaminated water sources to survive. In the name of profit, these corporate practices kill thousands of people per day from waterborne diseases. Roughly half the population of the developing world suffers from one or more of the six leading illnesses associated with poor water sanitation. The private sector has turned this nourishing resource into a commodity, and in the process, diminished the quality of water and depleted our environmental resources. We must return control of the most vital resource to the hands of the public to prevent the destruction of land, livelihoods, and lives.

The Corporate Empire:
The United States of America

Of the world's 100 richest institutions, 51 are corporations, and 47 of them are based in the United States of America. I would go so far as to say that America itself is a corporation at the heart of the financial system that controls the global economy. The United States constitutes only five percent of the world's population, yet consumes 25% of its resources, emits 30% of the world's pollution, and has the largest national debt at $27.2 trillion as of November 2, 2020. The United States also has the most powerful military in the world, which is why it is constantly involved in wars. Most of the nation's conflicts are little more than an opportunity for corporations to steal resources while they rebuild the country's infrastructure and earn an enormous profit. The United States has intentionally overthrown governments and instigated revolutions, coups, and assassinations all over the world wherever control of resources has become the main objective. The media then mobilizes to pump out stories of terrorism or threats to national security in order to justify these wars. This task is often seamlessly carried out, since the heads of large corporations that greatly benefit from these wars also own media and advertisement companies. These news outlets protect their own interests rather than impartially informing the public, and with the majority of people already distracted by the struggles of their own lives or social media and TV events, the average citizen does not often feel the true impact of these conflicts.

For thousands of years, vast empires have destroyed other nations and killed or enslaved their populations. The US is a relatively new civilization, and unlike those of the past, this empire possesses nuclear weapons and spends hundreds of millions of dollars per year on its global army. The manner in which the United States claims to be the ambassador of democracy in the world, yet rules through military force and subjugation is rather alarming, since the ideologies of democracy and imperialism directly conflict. Due to advancements in technology, the US military industrial complex has the capability to intervene in any global conflict by dispatching troops or CIA agents from any one of its 800 military bases around the world, yet the majority of US citizens are completely oblivious to the injustices their government commits on a daily basis. Those aware either ignore it and continue with their lives, believing that no solution can be found for such a seemingly insurmountable problem, or are deluded into thinking that their lifestyles do not contribute to it. The results of the political interventions, misuse of technology, and wastefulness are not often directly experienced in the Western world, and many find it difficult to see a connection between themselves and a person on the other side of the globe who bears the brunt of these consequences.

Having lived in America for nine years, I met numerous individuals who were genuinely kind people, but experienced high levels of stress and dissatisfaction with their lives. As a young man, I easily became caught up in the excitement of the American lifestyle, but after several years, the friends whose company I had previously enjoyed so often began to work overtime to earn money for houses, phones, cars, and an endless list of objects. They seemed to prefer spending time alone with their pets or technological devices rather than establishing meaningful connections with others, and I believe this left them with a sense of isolation in the long run. Enjoying hobbies, creating art, asking meaningful questions, or establishing sincere connections with others are made to seem unimportant compared to accumulating money. Instead, it becomes all about individuality and the plastic world of film stars, social media, and material objects. Genuine relationships are replaced with imaginary characters on phones and televisions, and the lack of authentic connections with real human beings breeds nothing but stress and unhappiness.

The Fictional World of Television

Our minds cannot distinguish between what we see on television and what occurs in real life, because the brain is wired to learn from its environment and the people in it. The brain then shapes a model of the world based on the information it processes regarding needs, emotions, ideas, and behavior. Children left in the company of television or the internet from a young age often continue this road their entire lives, and as adults, seem to prefer spending more time with pretend characters on their screens than with real people in the real world.

But what is so compelling about the characters on these screens? The brain fails to understand that these actors are not portraying genuine human experiences or reactions to real scenarios. Research in neuroscience concerning the brain's interaction with the outside world has yielded interesting results: the brain maps and experiences the reality through emotions, but it cannot discern between a genuine experience and an imagined scenario. Scientists connected patients to PET scanners to read their cerebral responses, and the patients were asked to look at an object, and then close their eyes and imagine that same object. In both cases, the same areas of the brain were stimulated, demonstrating that the brain has no way of discerning between what is real and what is imagined, and that our resulting thoughts concretely affect our perception of reality.

For years and years, we spend countless hours with on-screen characters portraying unrealistic emotions, situations, behavior, and body types. Our intellect does not comprehend that each actor has been carefully selected to play their role, and every single word has been written and rehearsed endlessly before all the scenes are perfectly shot and expertly edited. These scenarios are not based in reality, yet our brain wants to attain similar prestige, so we begin to think that something must be missing from our lives, causing us to feel sad and unfulfilled. As we use these electronic substitutes to replace real human interactions, attainable goals, and sincere emotions, we become more and more dissociated from reality and humanity.

Several years ago, I made a conscious choice to permanently turn off the television, and this allowed me to learn a great deal about the universe, the amazing biodiversity of our planet, the problems humanity faces, and our possible solutions. I have been able to travel to ten countries, learn two new languages, make many friends from all over the world, and volunteer with more than a dozen schools and foundations. I have been able to grow, challenge myself, and experience so much of this wonderful world, but I would not have been able to accomplish these goals if I had not made the conscious decision to quit polluting my mind on television, or another equally destructive form of entertainment—social media.

Social Media Syndrome

Social media, or as I prefer to call it, 'unsocial media,' is one of the most destructive forces to ever infect our interactions. Granted, the use of some social media can be beneficial, such as its use as an unbiased platform for citizens of oppressive countries, or for keeping in touch with distant friends and family, but in general, it has come to be used as a substitute for our important connections. Rather than spending time with someone face-to-face—fully connecting and engaging with them as we have evolved to do—we sit on our computers and cell phones communicating with people through texts, photos, and shaky videos. In any communal location, you now find people staring into their phones rather than paying attention to anyone or anything around them. In metros, buses, cafés, restaurants, parks, bars, clubs, and other public places where people ought to be interacting and connecting, social media has now taken over.

When I was younger, smartphones were not yet popular, and when I used to walk into a café or hostel, one of the first things I noticed was the loud hum of everyone mingling and chatting. But today those same places feel quiet because people hardly even look at each other, let alone have a conversation, because they are too busy staring at their phones. No matter where you go these days, you see nothing but people snapping pictures and selfies to post on

162

their social media accounts and show thousands of other people they don't know a curated concept of how good of a time they are having, even if it does not reflect their real experience.

It seems that people cannot go more than a few minutes without checking their phones, even when friends are right in front of them. Some spend hours taking the perfect picture and making numerous enhancements before posting it online. There is a Pavlovian satisfaction that comes with receiving a large number of likes, and a sense of personal insignificance without them, causing those who pay a great deal of attention to social media applications and websites to fall into destructive cycles of jealousy. Many people have lost themselves in this digital world of madness and competition, yet I personally do not care what you eat or where you go to take photos of yourself; I care about who you are as a person and what you are doing for other human beings and life on our planet. People spend more time on social media pretending that their lives are amazing, which sets up a world of false perfection, when in reality, we all have flaws, and that is just fine. We ought to leave this robotic realm behind and return to interacting with and relying upon one another as imperfect human beings, since this is who we truly are as a species.

Our Separation from Nature

Open your eyes and look around you. Are you in a manufactured space with four walls in a room filled with lifeless objects, most of which are unnecessary? Examine your surroundings and see if you sense a connection to your environment. When you have finished, step outside and look around. How much of nature, if any, do you see or hear? Gaze up to the sky above, take a deep breath, and fill your lungs with air that has existed for billions of years. Contemplate your relationship with this natural world that you did not create, but instead, created you. Now recall which of these environments you have dedicated your life to. Do you live within a society as rigid as the concrete upon which it was built, or do you live on an intricate, biological complex called Earth that is teeming with life, suspended in an infinite universe?

We now live in an age where the majority of humans are routinely encased in concrete environments, completely fixated on high-tech gadgets. As such, we have grown increasingly detached from our true selves and from the reality of our existence. We have become disconnected from the Earth because we are so occupied with technological inventions that our relationships with nature and one another have become fragmented. We have been placed in a small bubble constructed by the monetary society and conditioned to follow it blindly. Stop and ask yourself these questions:

Does your car, phone, TV, house, and material objects give you life? No they do not. Do the series, TV shows, and movies you watch or the social media you are plunged into give you life? No they do not. Does money give you life? No it does not, it gives you access to buy water and food that in turn give you life (please note that you can get water and food without money if you choose to do so). You are devoting everything to a world that does not give you life, while ignoring and destroying the natural world that, in fact, gives you life. Can you see something wrong with that? You belong to nature, but you have been uprooted and placed into a world of delusions

Humanity is currently controlled by ignorant, competitive, self-serving, and greedy killers. Take a step back and see what is happening on this planet from war, starvation, and destruction of nature and you will see this clearly. These monsters control us through the monetary system we are born into, as well as the brand of religion we are given. By blindly following them, we become just like them without even knowing it. We must truly understand that this global financial system has been created solely to earn money for those who already own most of the world's wealth. We must pause and learn about the history of this distressing financial system we live in, and then look at the world around us in order to consciously choose how we wish to live our lives thereafter.

Even though we may not be fully aware of it, our mundane actions have serious and deadly consequences, not only for other people in all parts of the world, but also for the diverse natural life this planet holds. Though modern societies condone taking much more than we actually need, we are collectively responsible for the damage inflicted upon our planet. Ignoring the consequences of this destruction does not lessen our individual responsibility; each of us must learn to develop a sense of global morality and protect the future of our species and life on our planet. To do so, we must find ourselves in the natural world, and come to the realization that humanity is just a drop of water in the ocean of reality. We need to evolve our thought process to a level where we really understand that we are not only human beings, but also life forms that are a part of Earth and the universe.

Every atom that composes your body, even the air you breathe, the food you eat, and the water you drink do not come from you. You would not exist if it were not for life itself. Should you not then dedicate your time and energy toward what gives you life? When you realize that everything you are is because of everything outside of you, you will clearly see that what created you and sustains your existence is, in fact, so beautiful. The universe is magical and the Earth and all its creatures are mesmerizing. Once you grasp the incredible fact that you come from these

166

amazing phenomena, you will be inspired to do something beautiful and incredible in turn. Dedicate your life to being involved with life itself and realize that by enhancing it, you will enhance yourself as well. You will excel in all facets of your life since you are plugged into the source of who you are. You will appreciate other people more when you see that they bring you everything you need to survive. You will be grateful for everything in nature because you know you are not here without it. Hopefully, you will then develop empathy for other human beings and life on our planet, which will connect you to all of humanity and the world at large, and you will then be part of the real story of life.

167

CHAPTER SIX

THE PHILOSOPHER

The Philosopher

One does not need to attend school to attain the mind of a philosopher—one must only be a seeker of truth and lover of wisdom. Philosophizing is a natural characteristic of the human experience and entails asking oneself profound and intimidating questions. It also requires a great deal of discipline and courage to face facts, however contradictory they may be to our personal beliefs. Philosophy promotes critical thinking and the opportunity to discover how much we really do not know, instilling us with a sense of humility. It gives us the incentive to explore, ask questions, and accept new answers obtained through rigorous investigation.

Truth and the Examined Life

The truth is a philosophical concept that must be tested through observation, reason, and measurable facts. It requires setting aside one's beliefs in an honest investigation of reality through the lens of logic. The truth exists in the objective evidence discovered through scientific experimentation and data collection. At the same time, science does not claim to have the answers to everything, but instead demonstrates that we are just beginning to understand the nature of the world around us. Science represents an exploration of our consciousness in order to discover facts that can be separated from subjective opinions.

Every single one of us possesses a consciousness that has been influenced by the environmental stimuli of the society in which we grew up. These social constructs determine how we perceive and approach real-world interactions. Our views of the world are initially shaped by the people who raise us, but as we grow older, we begin to think for ourselves and formulate our own beliefs. With every belief we acquire, we must always leave room for dispute and revision. As human beings, we ought to attempt to learn about the nature of reality by collecting evidence, testing it, and drawing conclusions from the results. In short, the scientific method leads the way in the quest for the truth, as this process is connected to the inquisitive nature of humans. Conversely, adopting social, religious, and monetary constructs conflicts with our nature because we forfeit our ability to ask questions and come to our own conclusions as intelligent human beings.

Before discussing the importance of self-reflection, I wish to give tribute to Socrates, since he truly believed that we had not only the right, but the duty to reflect upon our lives, examine our principles, and stand by our beliefs. He urged individuals not to conform to the status quo, compared people that blindly follow their leaders to sheep, and is remembered for the phrase: "An unexamined life is not a life worth living." Eventually charged with corrupting the minds of the youth and disrespecting the Greek gods, he was forced to drink hemlock and died. One of his most valuable legacies is a brilliant five-step method to arrive at the truth, and it still stands the test of time today:

- 1. Find a statement considered to be true.
- 2. Try to discover an exception to that rule.
- 3. If you find an exception, this means your statement is either false or imprecise.
- 4. Rethink your statement with the exception(s) in mind.
- 5. Continuously search for exceptions and model your statement accordingly.

Using this system of logic, the truest statement is one without exception (or very few exceptions) to these rules, and is therefore extremely difficult to disprove. If we could all reason in this manner, the beliefs we hold would be solid, and our perspective would be as close to the truth as possible. Socrates encouraged us to engage in open philosophical discussions, and taught us that it is our responsibility to base our decisions upon facts rather than opinions.

In modern societies, we find ourselves surrounded by buildings, technologies, social media, and far-fetched television shows. Add to that religion, money, and the endless stimuli running through our brains daily, and we have a recipe for disaster. Amidst this chaos, it is essential to pause to examine the natural order of things and what being alive on Earth really means. Explore the universe, the planet you are on, and the nature around you. Study the evolution of life and humanity, and evaluate your role in it. Scrutinize what exists concretely and what has been fabricated by our society's devotion to its religious and financial systems. Though the majority of us are completely oblivious to their existence, we have been immersed in these mechanisms from the moment we were born, and they control our lives to this day. We cannot go on blindly accepting the negative consequences our lives produce for others while there is a chance to examine and change our ways.

Being Wrong is Actually Right

Why is being wrong so frowned upon by society? Being wrong, becoming aware of it, and revising our outlook means that we are learning new information. Yet from an early age, we are conditioned to look down upon mistakes, and many individuals carry this mindset into adulthood, refusing to change their views about reality in order to feel that they hold the correct beliefs. It is perfectly ordinary to make mistakes and we must accept our fallibility as humans. We have to use reason and scientific study to discover who we are as a species in order to understand the path that brought us to where we are today. By doing so, we will be able to realize our potential to become a positive influence in the reality we all belong to.

The religious and financial structures do nothing but seek to control us as we struggle to make sense of the world and our purpose in it, which unfortunately has become increasingly related to accumulating money and material objects that have no positive aspects in our lives or the lives of others. We are too afraid to discover that we are part of a corrupt system, but questioning our social constructs is the only way to improve upon them. Never allowing anything to challenge our beliefs leads to an ignorant and static way of thinking and behaving. By enhancing our analytical skills, we can become more connected with the true reality of life.

The Ego

A mature philosopher uses the power of reason and logic to comprehend the ego, which seems to embody an animalistic survival mechanism directed toward self-preservation. The ego causes us to become conceited, competitive, and believe that we must stand out from others. The more we feed the ego with self-serving motives, the more it grows, separating us from reality and triggering dangerously destructive behaviors. By monitoring and controlling the ego, we are able to see ourselves as members of humanity, and by extension, all life on Earth and the universe that contains it. We become humble and open to learning what it really means to be part of reality. If we can leave our egos behind, we become more open to change and progress toward becoming more positive, intelligent, inspired, and creative individuals constantly looking to better ourselves as well as others.

We must strip away the layers of selfish and subjective ideas that we have accumulated throughout our lives and observe the objective reality revealed to us by observation and analysis. Science has provided us with an understanding of the inner workings of our physiology, but we must also take a look at our philosophical side. If you think critically, logically, and morally, you are already a philosopher, which is simply an innate part of being human. Through the marriage of science and philosophy, we can begin to comprehend our consciousness as an incredible gift that helps us appreciate the true beauty and value of our lives.

Our consciousness is part of the evolutionary process and never stops expanding. Examining our humble beginnings and what our species has become, along with our individual place in the world, is a vital undertaking. Once we acquire this knowledge, we can scientifically and philosophically consider how the human creations of the religious and monetary systems fit into reality.

By studying the world's selfishness, suffering, and greed, you come to understand that these are all products of the monetary and religious systems. Hopefully, you will be able to free yourself from these destructive confines and awaken to empower yourself through the many positive human aspects you possess. You can then begin to understand that you are a part of a larger world in which you can make positive changes, since the actions you are currently taking are likely on the negative side of the equation.

During this journey of reinventing yourself and uncovering your true purpose, you will encounter moments of despair, doubt, and weakness. The world is filled with countless obstacles, and today it is harder than ever to live an honest, meaningful, and selfless life. However, always return to the tools you possess as a genuine human being, and though you may become discouraged along the way, trust that you are traveling a noble path.

The Moral Self

Morality shapes our construct of that which is good and that which is bad. It helps us discern from right and wrong, not only in the things we do, but also in the things we *do not* do. We exercise morality in the choices we make every day, but we must comprehend just how powerful and

175

influential these decisions can be in our world. Each individual ought to strive to be a part of making the world a better place to live, which can include assisting the poor, preserving endangered animals, or becoming an advocate for truth, human rights, and freedom.

It is possible for the majority of the pain, misery, and suffering in war-torn and impoverished regions—a product of the monetary system of greed and power—to be avoided entirely. Water, food, and medicine are available for everyone, yet billions of people are unable to afford these basic needs simply because they were born in a region of the world that has been exploited by the system and robbed of its resources. When we see injustice in another part of the world on our screens, it is easy to not feel much empathy for our fellow human beings because they have no direct impact on our lives. However, this outlook represents one of the greatest moral issues of modern times, and it is important to remember that the family, country, and cultural mindset into which you were born were all simply a matter of blind luck. With this realization, you truly become human and gain a sense of responsibility for the unnecessary suffering of your brothers and sisters.

The human brain evolved to create empathetic, social, and caring creatures, yet we tend to operate with the primitive part of the brain, making us nothing more than walking, talking animals governed by opportunistic, self-serving, and competitive characteristics. Three important sections of our brain function symbiotically to drive our consciousness and analytical abilities, with the brain stem as its primitive foundation. This 300-million-year old reptilian part of the brain is responsible for keeping us awake and alert, engaging the body's fight-or-flight mechanism, and maintaining involuntary organ function such as heartbeat and respiration. The limbic system—or mammalian brain—is a 200 million-year-old structure responsible for emotions, memory, pleasure, and reward. Along with the brain stem, all mammals rely upon the limbic system to navigate situations that involve reasoning, processing new information, and personal preferences.

The third part of our brain is known as the frontal cerebral cortex. This part of the brain is unique to hominids and drives consciousness, cognition, and speech. Around two million years ago, our brain developed a larger prefrontal cortex than that of our hominid ancestors, and researchers have often used this size discrepancy to explain the wide range of differences in human personalities, cultures, and character traits. This section of the brain helps us read the emotions of others, and it is the hub of our morality, mindfulness, and self-awareness.

Understanding the inner workings of our brain enables us to adjust our thoughts and behaviors to improve our lives as well as the lives of those around us. The

177

religious and monetary systems of today's societies thrive upon keeping us locked in the primitive brain, but the key to rediscovering our unique sense of humanity lies in the enhancement of the neuron circuitry in the prefrontal cortex region, since a mind that utilizes this part of the brain is more likely to be morally sound, altruistic, enthusiastic, and content.

Moral human attributes such as cooperation and kindness played a large role in human evolution by increasing our chances of survival from the time we were primates. We had never been loners, but we have now been warped into individualistic beings functioning—or rather malfunctioning—in our contemporary capitalist societies. We have been made to feel as though we must accumulate more material objects to experience happiness, since our human connections have broken down. Simply asking for help is thought of as a sign of dependence and looked down upon, even though we are a social species that has relied upon one another throughout history to survive.

Our ability to cooperate is one of the most important evolutionary constructs that aided human survival, but financial institutions have turned us into loners, creating a void in our consciousness that this system attempts to fill with God, material objects, or on-screen brainwashing. In the harsh and ever-changing conditions from which we evolved, living a solitary life was surely a death sentence, and it is the same today, at least from a psychological standpoint.

If humans had not evolved a sense of morality, affection, and respect, we would not have been able to live in groups for survival. Without these principles, humanity will certainly be obliterated, yet our species is already heading in that direction. These communal values have been replaced by animalistic, predatory, and competitive instincts, leading to separation and self-destruction.

The time has come to wake up and examine the choices we make, as well as how they adversely affect the system of life which allowed us to exist on this planet. The fact that we are destroying the very nature that created us and rendering the Earth a less inhabitable place for generations to come is highly unconscionable. We ought to make a positive impact on the people and life that share this planet with us, which will allow us to exercise our true moral self.

Reality and Existence

Since we clearly exist, *something* must contain that existence. Is it a narrow-minded materialistic society built of plastic and concrete, which blinds you to reality? Or do you exist in a universe that is 13.8 billion years into its evolution on a planet full of life and beauty? Every one of us obviously exists on Earth, but have you come to truly realize this fact? The universe created you and everything around you, yet society limits your existence to materialistic objectives. Above you, a sun has been around for five billion years, the planet you live on is 4.6 billion years old, and the biological life process that created you has been evolving for the last 3.8 billion years. Rarely do we reflect upon these wonders because our minds are cluttered with the details of a detrimental and deadly lifestyle. We must always remind ourselves where we live, what supports our existence, and what role each of us plays in this world.

Our concrete-based civilization does not concern itself with animals, trees, water, the natural world, or what its social structures are doing to our brothers and sisters in other parts of the world. We may not comprehend (or may choose to ignore) the fact that people in the poor areas of the world are exploited to support our materialistic existence, but it happens every second of every day. Modern societies completely contradict nature and our natural way of life because they are directed solely toward selfish motives and the desire to attain possessions.

The objective of humanity ought to be dedicated to an evolution of consciousness to reconnect with nature. In order to fully comprehend that you are a living being in the universe, you must disconnect from the binds of society and gain some understanding of the natural world. Once this door opens, it exposes a true image of a meaningful reality, and the key to unlocking this door lies in scientific and philosophical knowledge. I must honestly say that it takes time and hard work to achieve a sense of truth; however, trust that through any confusion you may experience, you are becoming part of the true reality.

Perspective

Our perspective in life is the most powerful tool driving our purpose, and it is a direct product of the information we have accumulated over the course of our lives. Blindly following this destructive system does not even scratch the surface of what it means to be human. Society fuels our fearful, predatory, and competitive sides, causing us to live unhappy lives with a retracted self. Studying science and philosophy expands our awareness to connect with the web of life on our planet, and our positive selves become fulfilled. I am not advising anyone to leave their job, disassociate from civilization, and live in the wild—it is possible to retain your profession and wealth, but I implore you to discover who you are outside of societal constructs.

Apart from our basic needs, we ought to dedicate the rest of our time to becoming positive influences on this planet, but we will not be able to do so through the misuse of technology or other excessively harmful behaviors. There needs to be a universal awakening of the self and an expansion of our individual perspective. We must tap out of our shallow perceptions and realize that we are one life form interconnected to an infinite number of others. It is time to understand that we have a responsibility to all life on this planet and that our actions affect the rest of humanity and the environment that sustains us. Giving back to what is truly valuable allows us to feel more enlightened and content. As we shed the layers we have accumulated of the destructive, hypnotic lifestyle we have led, we begin to experience our true selves—kind, giving, and generous. However, it is impossible to become this person in a limited routine where one remains stagnant, dormant, selfish, and negative.

I truly believe that the only way we can fully realize ourselves is through studying our natural reality because scientific study opens the door to our connection with nature. Philosophical and rational thought are characteristics unique to human beings and separate us from all other creatures on this planet. If you cannot appreciate these innate aspects of humanity, you are nothing but an animal no different than any other creature driven to kill, eat, and procreate

The Explorer in Each of Us

Human beings have been designed to investigate, if only for the fact that we are the only species on our planet with the ability to both ask and answer the question "why?" Not only have we explored the farthest reaches of our planet and solar system, humans have also searched for the answers to complex questions about the universe and the meaning of life. We live in a precarious age of information and technology where it is more pertinent than ever for us to explore our own faults as well as strengths in order to save our species from the dangerous and irresponsible course we are traveling.

Modern society has stripped us of the power to wonder and think for ourselves, leaving our brains susceptible to escaping into the pretend world of social media and television. We have lost the ability to intellectually investigate our surroundings, believing that there is nothing more to life than supporting the monetary and religious systems society imposes upon us. We must regain our exploratory selves and return to who we truly are—passionate human beings motivated by curiosity and the pursuit of knowledge.

What is Humanity?

Are we living entities that exist to try to endlessly impress one another by posting, reading, and sharing photos of the places we go, parties we attend, and the clothes or shoes we wear? Are we really only interested in these tasteless and meaningless displays? Can this really be all that humanity amounts to? Or can it involve demonstrating nobility, sacrifice, perseverance, compassion, and morality, as well as advancing our species, and taking care of the life around us? Are we not explorers of mountains, forests, oceans, the furthest reaches of our planet, and the very universe itself? Are we not scientists, artists, dreamers, thinkers, and creators of medicine and technology?

Ask yourself what kind of a human being you are— one who wakes up to repeat the same meaningless routine every day, feeling disenchanted and glued to a digital screen, or one who plays an active role in improving the world around them and understands what it means to be human? I encourage you to go beyond the scope of what is taught in school and study the history of humanity from the time we evolved on the plains of Africa to the present day. Discover how human beings—the first species in the 3.8-billion-year history of life to revolutionize this planet—fought and survived against all odds. Once you realize who we are as a collective species, you will gain a greater understanding of who you are as an individual, and how you are capable of achieving amazing and significant accomplishments in this world.

One way to awaken your sense of humanity is to travel at every available opportunity, with the intention of taking in the diversity of life from different cultures, people, mindsets, natural beauty, and amazing architecture that we have built throughout history. Rather than cycling through the same familiar activities (visiting fancy hotels, restaurants, bars, coffee shops, etc.) as you do in your hometown, spend time in the heart of the country where you will be able to experience the local culture. It is essential to appreciate how different other societies may be from your own and come to the realization that there is no "correct" or "right" one. Each and every culture around the world represents a unique part of humanity to be appreciated. *This* is how we truly learn who we are as human beings, rather than boasting about the objects that we or other people own. We all belong to a universe, to a planet, and to life itself; and we therefore all have an obligation to better humanity and the world we share.

Responsibility

Surely the responsibility for the future of the species and life on this planet falls upon all of us, but it falls especially upon every individual in the Western, wealthy, and developed world, since the actions and decisions of these populations drive this system, whether its citizens know it or not. We are the ones responsible (through our purchases, lifestyle, dependence on fossil fuels, etc.) for the suffering and subjugation of the less fortunate and the overuse of resources that leads to the destruction of the natural world. Instead of numbly participating in this devastation, we can choose instead to be a part of the solution. Once we see how we all contribute to an oppressive system, a sense of responsibility begins to arise, as does the understanding that for every action there is a reaction. We are conscious beings capable of contemplating the majesty of the universe, curing diseases, traveling through space, and helping any other person or animal if we choose to do so, and it is up to the individuals in the more developed nations to step up and make a difference.

To be responsible is to take accountability for your actions and understand that they have a greater impact on the world at large, not to mention the countless species that make their home here. It means genuinely considering whether you are here on Earth to feed into the destructive, wasteful, and ignorant part of humanity, or to choose decency, kindness, and curiosity. I encourage you to contemplate the answers to the following questions:

- Which species is responsible for the greatest number of extinctions of other species on this planet?

- Which species causes unnecessary death and suffering for the members of its own species?

- Which species pollutes, poisons, and destroys all other life on the planet?

- Do you consider yourself a conscious being, a member of this species, and part of life on this planet?

- Do you believe that you contribute to the death and destruction of your brothers and sisters, as well as other life forms?

- Does ignoring this fact absolve you of its terrible effects?

- What role do you play on this planet and in this system of life?

- Do you feel driven to find significance in this world in an honorable way?

- Do your actions—both positive and negative—have a meaningful impact on the world?

- Can you make a difference, however small, to reduce your negative impact and help the less fortunate members of humanity?

- If you became part of the solution instead of the problem, would your existence not be more significant to all life on this planet?

When you take responsibility for the destructive aspects of modern civilization and find your purpose on this planet, you will return power to your own hands. You will experience a change of perspective from "*they* ought to solve the problem" to "*I* ought to be the one working toward a solution." You will then start to comprehend the negative role you play in the world and begin to steer yourself toward a more positive one. Your contributions will make you feel that you are a part of the solution and trying your best to minimize the problem. Your priorities will become clearer, your outlook on the world will improve, and you will become a happier person.

The Three Paradigms

As members of the human species, every one of us belong to one of three potential paradigms: the neutral, the problem, or the solution. Under the neutral paradigm, the actions of a human being do not contribute to the problem or the solution. A tribe member removed from society and its technologies makes an excellent example—such an individual neither adds to nor subtracts from the problem, as they do not cause the indirect pollution, death, and destruction to nature and fellow human beings with their actions. This individual is likewise relieved from responsibility, since they possess no knowledge of the societal construct in which we live, and therefore has no obligation to become part of the solution.

Under our current social and monetary system, two categories of individuals fall under the problem paradigm. The first type does not know that they are a part of the problem, and include the poor, uneducated, and malnourished victims of society and its monetary system. They are born fending for their lives in the search for basic human needs such as shelter, food, and clean water. This group does not know that they are contributing to the problem by misusing society's technologies, and even if they did, they do not have the means or knowledge to reach much of a solution. The second type of individual under the problematic paradigm make up a great majority of the populations of the developed nations and knowingly contribute to or actively ignore the dilemma. They are capable of contributing to the solution, but choose not to because of a self-centered perspective. I also include hypocrites in this category—those who discuss what *others* ought to do without taking any real action themselves. A member of the solution paradigm aims to become a part of the solution for all life on the planet. These people perceive the problem, recognize that they are a part of it, and contribute to a solution.

For many years, I was an example of the second individual in the problem paradigm, until the moment I could no longer hide from or ignore how my behavior impacted the world. I knew that I had to take responsibility for my passive participation in this destructive society and join the solution paradigm in order to minimize my negative impact on life on this planet.

189

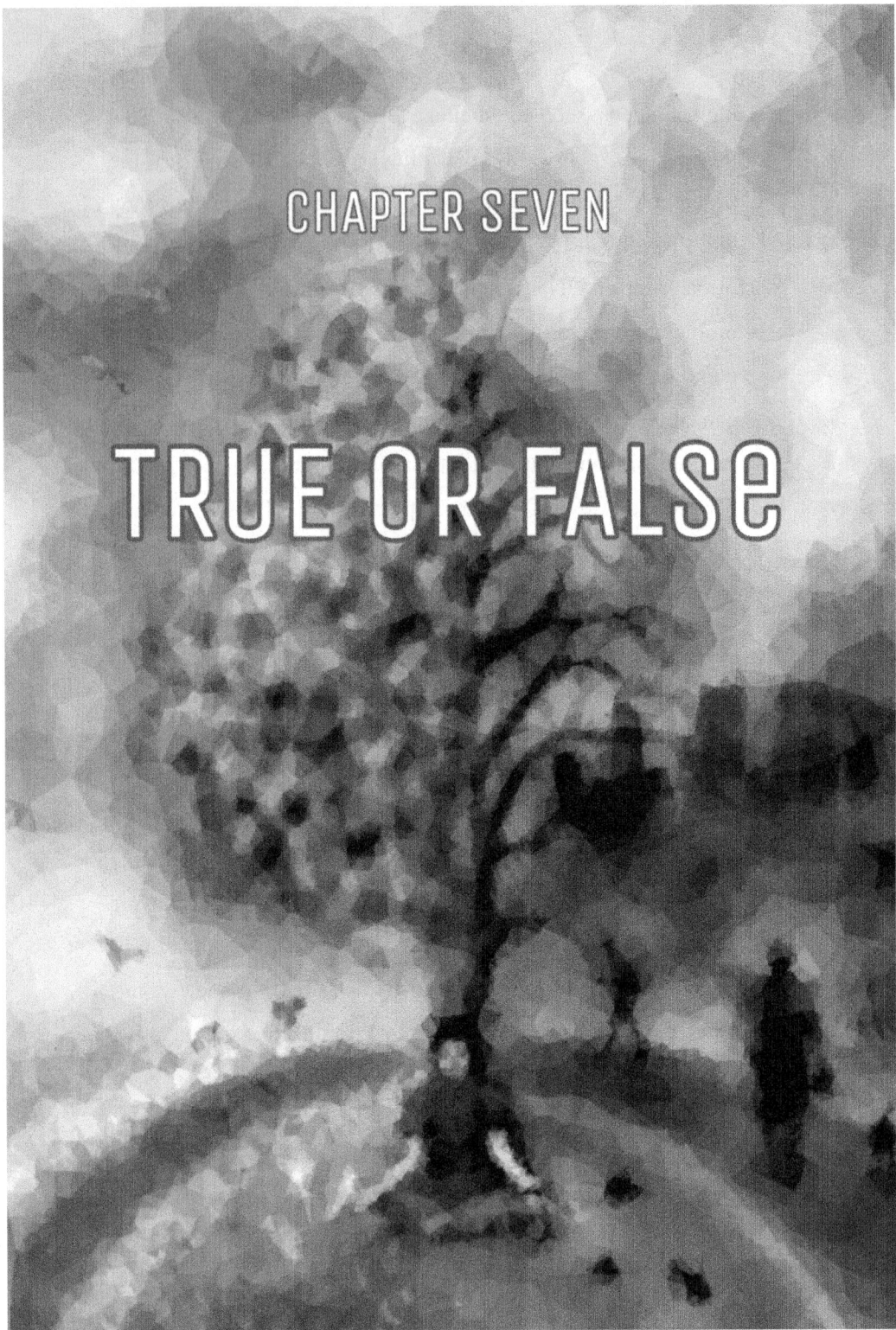

CHAPTER SEVEN

TRUE OR FALSE

True or False

The Objective Truth

In this final chapter, I invite you to be the philosopher and argue with me about the validity and truthfulness of every single word that you will read. Ask yourself questions about my analysis and if you find my statements to be objectively true, then you must adopt these truths into your life. We have to look outside ourselves and our subjective views and see that there is a truth that exists outside of our personal opinions. As much as the objective truth is attainable, it is evident that it is something we cannot argue about, and that all human beings in existence can agree on. For example, we have to drink water to survive, we live on a planet, the sun gives everything life on Earth, etc. In contrast, a subjective truth is based on personal opinion or preference. For example, red is the most beautiful color, Christianity is the one and only true religion, cats are cuter than dogs, etc. There are 7.8 billion people in the world and 7.8 billion subjective truths. However, there is one and only one objective truth, and this is what we need to align ourselves with.

Let us start with mathematics. Math is poetically referred to by many scientists as being the language of the universe, which means that by using it humans are speaking with the universe and learning about it. We have been using math to ask the universe many questions since the dawn of our evolution, and its answers have been very clear and 100% true. 1+1=2 is a true answer and as much as you want it to be 3, 4, or 5 it will never be. If you go to buy a bottle of water at the store that costs $2 and you pay with a $5 bill, how much should your change be? If the cashier gives you back $2, then you can, with absolute certainty tell them that they are wrong. If the cashier gives you back $3, and you tell them that they need to give you back $4, then they can tell you with absolute certainty that you are wrong. There is only one true answer and all the other answers are wrong. Math can only answer with two responses either true or false. Through math, the universe has only told us the truth, and made us understand that it cannot be wrong, but rather only people with their subjective opinions can be wrong.

Following mathematics to attain the objective truth—which removed human fallibility from the equation— we now had a clear method to ask the universe questions and obtain the correct answers. As such, we have used math to discover that the universe has physical laws that we have labeled as physics. Physics taught us that the universe is made out of matter and energy that constitute everything in reality. Through the laws of physics we were able to understand how matter and energy formed all the galaxies, stars, planets, us, and everything else in the universe. All matter is formed by atoms, and by learning about how these atoms interact, combine, and change into new compounds, another branch in our knowledge of the universe arose, chemistry. We then soon realized that the natural process of physics and chemistry combined to create life on our planet, and thus the field of biology was born. Math, physics, chemistry, and biology became the bases of what we refer to as science with all its different branches. Those four disciplines have taught us about how the universe functions and have given us a clear method in how to find the truth. I am talking about the scientific method that has given us all the true knowledge that we possess about the world today. Using science to investigate the truth of our universe, we were able to create absolutely everything that we see in our society today. Buildings, houses, roads, cars, airplanes, computers, phones, televisions, refrigerators, air conditions, tables, chairs, beds, shoes, clothes, lights, and countless other gadgets that are part of human ingenuity. Science has also brought water into your home, along with food into your supermarkets and restaurants. Science offered you hospitals and countless medicines to treat your fragile biology, and so many technologies used in surgeries and other medical needs that could save your life. The truth of the universe through science is very evident in your everyday life although you might not even give it one thought. If you don't think science is true—take off your clothes, leave everything man-made behind, and walk barefoot to the closest forest and think about it. The knowledge we possess so far about the objective truth of the universe has given us everything we rely on today, but unfortunately most of us are oblivious to it all. The human inventions that we are so occupied with are just the tip of the iceberg of what science has offered us.

The greatest gift that science has given us is the understanding that we inhabit a universe 13.8 billion years in existence. This truth is the reason for everything which exists, including you and all the things we know and might not know yet. It is absolutely imperative for each one of us to take in this knowledge, to humble ourselves, and learn from the universe that created us. It has given us absolutely everything, including the gift to learn from it by following math, physics, chemistry, and biology.

Now, allow me to plant you back into the universe that you have been uprooted from:
- Where do you live?
First and foremost you live in your body.
- What is your body made out of?
It's made out of atoms of carbon, hydrogen, oxygen, nitrogen, calcium, phosphorus, and a few other elements which all come from the heart of stars that are in the universe.
- Where does your body stand, sit, walk, run, and sleep on?

On a planet we named Earth that is revolving around a star that we called the Sun, and both of them are suspended in the universe.

- What is the sun?

It's a ball of hydrogen and helium that produces light and heat which supports all life on Earth.

- What does your body need to survive?

It needs sunlight, air, water, and food. Sunlight comes from the sun, air is made out of nitrogen, oxygen and a small amount of other gasses. Water is made out of two atoms of hydrogen and one atom of oxygen, and food is carbon based life that has been evolving on our planet for billions of years.

- Are other life forms important for my existence?

First of all, you evolved from other life forms, you eat other life forms that you or other people kill for you. There are innumerous microbial life forms on and in your body that help you survive, and the oxygen that you breathe comes from photosynthetic life forms such as plants and trees.

I understand that these are simple truths, however we tend to not pay even the slightest attention to the fundamental reasons that we all exist. I urge you to take some time to contemplate that your atoms come from a universe 13.8 billion years into its evolution. Your atoms constitute your body, and your body is one biological entity out of countless others, all part of life that has been evolving on planet Earth for 3.8 billion years. You are a part of one species out of billions that exist and have existed and gone extinct. You are on a planet that is rotating on its axis with tremendous speeds. The Earth is revolving around a sun that has been here for five billion years, and which without, you and everything else in the solar system would not exist. The sun is flying around in a galaxy containing hundreds of billions of other stars and planets. Our galaxy is zipping through space along with hundreds of billions of other galaxies that contain hundreds of billions of stars and planets each. This is the most factual information we have about the truth of our existence. Do you understand the beauty and immensity of this reality that you are not even touching with your every day life by living in a mere insignificant speck that is your imagination, uprooted from and blinded to the grandeur of what you belong to?

In the first three chapters, I laid out important scientific information to show how much we factually know about the truth that we exist in. However, we live outside of this truth only in our minds because we were born in religion and the system that I detailed in chapters four and five. These two human inventions that are so far removed from the truth of our reality make us live in our imagination, while we miss out on the biggest truth that exists.

Religion and the system have placed us in a false and damaging construct where we are constantly in a state of stress, anxiety, suffering, and so much negativity, because we are living outside of nature, locked in an imaginary world. Just like a fish deprived of water, we live our lives cut off from what gives us life. The truth is simple—we live in a body made out of atoms that come from stars in the universe, we do stand on a planet, and we did evolve here just like all the other life forms we see around us, but in our minds we are living in two false human ideologies that block us from the truth while destroying us and the life around us. We need to start facing the facts and challenge their authenticity, but when we fail to do so, we must then accept the truth and align our lives with it. We have to adopt the truth into our lives and throw away the lies and the insignificance of our imagination.

Vicious Imagination

We all know that every human being has good and bad aspects. A good human being is selfless, honest, trustworthy, empathetic, compassionate, giving, helpful, and strives to create rather than destroy. A bad human being is self-centered, a liar, a murderer, untrustworthy, apathetic, heartless, power hungry, greedy, and destructive. We are animals just like any other creature on this planet; however what differentiates us from other organisms and makes us human beings are our good qualities. The bad attributes belong to a primitive animal that is only concerned with the self while disregarding everyone and everything else.

Let us now take a look at the objective truth about the characteristics of the human beings that have been running humanity for thousands of years. I urge you to make a comparison between how true, beautiful, and positive the universe is and how it has given you your life to live it freely without asking for anything in return, and how the system is one big lie full of destruction and negativity that imprisons you under its rule.

If we only take the last 500 years since the scientific revolution took off in Europe and see what has happened with humanity and the nature around us, then you will know what kind of animals are running the world and your life. Taking advantage of our brilliant scientific advancements, the heads of the system in Europe such as England, France, Spain, and Portugal took off to destroy and enslave all of humanity. These power hungry, greedy, and miserable killers wiped out millions upon millions of human beings from existence, and stripped the survivors from their freedom, culture, language, and their Gods and religions. And to expand their reign of terror, they enslaved so many people from the countries they ravaged, forced them into hard labor, and treated them like animals until they died. Have you ever wondered why today there are 67 countries that speak English, 29 that speak French, 20 that speak

Spanish, and 10 that speak Portuguese? These countries are now controlled by the heads of the system and their people speak the languages of their oppressors, believe in their God and religion, and produce so much profit for them.

I do not care who these monsters are nor do I care about their names. I am only observing the product of their rule, and the truth of who they are and what they are doing is very clear. In the last 100 years these "world leaders" have caused many wars, including two world wars, as they compete against each other for power. They sent us to fight their wars to murder each other for their benefit. They have placed us in interment camps, imprisoned us, tortured us, burned us alive, and dropped atomic bombs on us. They have made us suffer in sickness, famines, and thirst and separated us from each other through illusions of religions, nationalities, races, and financial classes.

Today, they are still here running the world as they wish, and sadly we are following them blindly as we are plugged into their system—doing what they want us to do and using what they gave us to use. They are taking advantage of our technological wonders to pollute and destroy nature so they can manufacture products to sell us. They have turned human society into blocks of concrete where all of our interactions seem to be between four walls full with their products. They have constructed a fake world for us to live in where we have to pay them money for absolutely everything. Take a minute to think about it, is there anything in this society that you do not pay for? I can only think of the air that we breathe that they have not yet found a way to charge us for. We are made to pay for water and food, and if you cannot afford it, then you can suffer and die. Every year, roughly 3.4 million people die from drinking contaminated water and nine million die of hunger. And of course, there are billions of other people in poverty barely surviving and suffering with illnesses related to contaminated water and malnutrition. And for the rest of humanity, we are forced to buy water without knowing its origin, and the food they send us is full of chemicals that make us sick. Furthermore, they create food and other products that play on the natural addictions of human beings with elements such as fat, sugar, caffeine, alcohol, and nicotine—so we can get addicted to their products and consume them. It seems that their goal is to keep us sitting down as inactive as possible, mostly between four walls separated from nature. From your bed to your chair, you consume their foods and watch their programs on your phone and TV. From your chair to your car where you listen to their news while you are driving to your job, where you will then sit for hours to make them money. After work, you repeat these steps in reverse back to your bed and the next day the cycle repeats itself. On the weekend, you either stay at home pumping your brain with misinformation from the

200

imaginary world they created for you on their screens, or drunk to excess to forget about it all. Because we are inactive and consuming bad food, water, air, and misleading information, most of us in this society have become both mentally ill and physically sick. We can pray to the God they gave us, but, unfortunately, he cannot help us as he is simply a figment of our imagination.

Stress, anxiety, fear, sadness, loneliness, depression, obesity, hypertension, type 2 diabetes, and high cholesterol are just a few of the medical disorders that arise in our bodies. Do not worry though, because they have more addictive chemicals in the form of pills to offer you for all your problems that they have given you, but of course you have to pay for them and get addicted to them for the rest of your life. You pay them for giving you the problem, and you pay them for giving you the fake remedy. The root of the problem, however, is the system itself.

In the USA 70% of the population is overweight and obese, and 66% of adults are on prescription drugs. Can we consider that the USA, which is the heart of the system, is concerned for the lives of the human beings living under its rule? Do you think a human being living in a tribe or village connected to nature and to the people in his community and growing his own food, experiences so many negative outcomes?

They have constructed this world and placed us in it, as they trap us in the beautiful gift that every human has which is their imagination. Spending so much time with television and its imaginary world and social media and its imaginary interactions further separates us from reality. It really needs to be understood that who you are is nothing but a collection of information you have gathered from your environment over your lifetime. The more true information you possess about the reality of your existence the better your brain and body function, while the more false information you acquire the more your brain and body malfunction.

Most of the processes happening in your brain are subconscious. Just imagine the limitless mechanisms happening in your body every moment that are keeping you alive that you don't control or even know about. The subconscious brain is learning from your environment at all moments. It takes in all the information that your five senses are subjected to—be it true or false—and gives it back to the conscious part of you to construct reality. In real life you might have 10-15 people that your brain is learning from, however, on your screen you have interacted with thousands of fake people. Although you might know that what you are watching is imaginary, your brain does not. Your brain absorbs this imaginary information and gives it back to you to use in your everyday life, which has nothing to do with the imaginary world. And as you spend countless hours with imaginary people you are deeply damaging your perception of the real world. Ask yourself what percentage of the scenarios and interactions between the characters that are depicted in the shows or movies you watch could happen in real life? Is it more than 1%? We must give our brain the correct information about reality so it can help us live in the real world because that is where we factually live. The system is trapping us in our imagination with our televisions and phones, while encasing us in concrete separated from real interactions with other human beings and the nature that contains us all. Which is more important, watching a person acting about an imaginary story that has never existed other than in the imagination of a writer and getting lost in an imaginary world, or staying in the truth of a universe which is beyond anyone's imagination? Which is more significant, to learn about and be involved in imagination or truth? Which of the two do you think would put you on a better path in your life?

Let us now examine religion through the lens of the objective truth. Since the beginning of humanity we have been creating Gods and religions, and today there are 4,200 religions—most having their own holy books and Gods. Can you imagine how many Gods and religions have been invented in the past 200,000 years of humanity's existence? If we only take a total of 10,000 Gods and religions, and assume that one could be correct, what are the chances that your God and religion are correct? The answer is 0.01%. If I place 10,000 bottles in front of you, and I tell you only one bottle contains water and the rest have poison in them that will kill you, would you make the decision to drink one? Would you take any decision in life based on those odds? However, you have unknowingly taken this decision with the God and religion you enslaved yourself under for a whole lifetime, although it has a likelihood of being 99.99% false.

I implore you to come back to reality. Where are these 10,000 Gods? Have you seen any of them in the real world? They are all in people's imagination. Different people in different places in the world and at different times have created different Gods and religions. The popular Gods and religions we have today are prevalent because we are here at this point in time, but they did not exist just a couple of thousand years ago. Today, because of wars and invasions, the dominate religions, including Christianity and Islam, have been imposed on populations of countries around the world that had other Gods and religions. For example, when Spain colonized most countries in South America, they destroyed the temples of the local indigenous religions, built churches instead, and forced the people to convert or die.

The objective truth relies on mathematical equations not stories of magic that claim to have broken the rules of math, physics, chemistry, and biology. According to the truth, there are no heavens, hells, talking animals, flying people, or any magic whatsoever, and I think this is very clear and evident in our everyday lives. Human beings are story tellers with a vivid imagination that unfortunately runs wild. It is easy to see this by taking a look at the limitless fictional stories created in novels, movies, TV shows, and religious books.

Imagining Gods and religions were a natural product of our ignorance and fear of the natural world, and the people running the world realized that they could capitalize on our weaknesses and control us while making more money throughout the process. Follow the teaching of this one and only true religion, don't dare to look elsewhere, and obey God's commandments or else you will be punished in this life and the next. Thus, you create this fictional character in your imagination. You fear him and obey him by doing what the people running the religion who wrote the books want you to do. One can easily see how the most popular religions today are some of the richest institutions in the world. They have tricked their believers into giving them money just like any other corporation that is part of the system. Lastly, if the heads of religions were good people following the good God that they had created, should they not be using every last penny of their trillions of dollars to give clean water and food to all the humans in need?

We are so stressed, unhappy, lazy, frustrated, feeling trapped under financial pressure, while our bodies are out of shape and our mental state follows. Why do we need to be this way? Is this at all how we are supposed to live? Is this a life that any other creature on earth is living? Would you wish this lifestyle and its toxicity on any other life form? Please notice that all other organisms on Earth live freely and vigorously, while we live with an illusion of freedom. The only other life forms that are not free are the ones we imprisoned as domesticated animals. If you live with the negative feelings that I mentioned above, the ones that weigh many people down, you cannot honestly tell me that you are really free. All the negative feelings you have are a result of a system based on bad and demonstrably false ideologies. If you free yourself from it and go back to your origin as a life form just like any other creature on this planet, you will be free just like they are.

The system makes us oblivious to the destruction we are causing to the nature that we depend on that keeps us alive. Every single human being on this planet, all 7.8 billion of us know at our core that we are destroying the nature we depend on. However we ignore the truth and distract ourselves with the imaginary world. If we were living in the real world, in nature, in "reality" that gives us life, that gives us the air, water, and food, then we will not ignore it but rather we would help it. The real world is beyond amazing

206

and beyond any adjective that we can come up with. The Earth and the millions of species that exist and have existed on it are unbelievable.

Please note that if any of the following life forms such as trees, insects, or worms disappear, life as we know it on this planet will die with it. But if human beings disappear, life on this planet will flourish in every corner of the Earth. If we compare ourselves to any other organism on Earth, we will quickly see how worthless we are to life itself. A tree for example, absorbs carbon dioxide that we produce and gives us and all other life forms oxygen to breathe. A tree gives shade to land creatures and serves as a home to many others. It gives its leaves and fruits for us and other organisms to eat while fertilizing the soil around it with the dead matter that falls from it.

Do you see how valuable a tree is to life on Earth? Now, let us examine our contribution. We pollute, trash, destroy, suck the life out of everything, and give nothing back in return. The only good we do for life is giving it our feces, and our bodies when we die, which are both unwilling actions. This is what we represent for life on Earth as we are plugged into this system. Why do we support and reward a system that is making us this way, while we ignore and destroy nature that has freely given us everything? We can play a very important and positive part in life, more so than many other organisms as we are so much more aware and capable. However, as long as we are drowning in our self-centeredness and imagination, we will remain negative and destructive until we die. We know of about 8.7 million species on our planet today, and every single organism belonging to these species is more valuable then every one of us.

We are supposedly, the most conscious species in the history of life on this planet, but I dare to differ, because as we live in our societies and in our imagination we are definitely not conscious about killing the life that gives us life. We are unconsciously driving millions of species into extinction because we are truly sick.

The system is a virus to life on the planet and every one of us is a cell of this virus bent on destruction. We currently are the worst species in the history of life on the planet for the simple fact that we are knowingly killing members of our own species along with numerous other species. We are in fact, driving ourselves into extinction while dragging 80-90% of all life on the planet down with us. If we continue on this path, we will go down as the first species in the 3.8 billion year history of Earth being dumb and arrogant enough to do that.

Human or Animal?

All members of the animal kingdom, including us, can kill, eat, drink, mate, sleep, lay down, waste time doing nothing at all, play, and protect and provide for themselves. There is nothing special or impressive at all about these functions. However, every animal has traits that makes it unique and differentiates it from other animals. For example a venomous snake has two long fangs that inject poison into its pray, extremely flexible jaws that allow it to eat a pray bigger than its head, infrared heat sensors, sensitivity to low-frequency ground vibrations, a quickness of attack, and more. So, what differentiates human beings from other animals? Brain power and high levels of consciousness portrayed in our logic, reason, symbolic abstract thinking, solving complex problems, language, art, science, and the use of tools to build structures and technologies. We possess advanced social skills depicted in cooperation, collaboration, morality, compassion, and empathy. We are upright walkers that can live in any climate on Earth, and our bodies have the endurance to run marathons, swim great distances, and climb the highest mountains. These are the traits that make us human, and without developing them in our lives I dare to say that we are but a simple animal. What happens if the snake gives away its traits or barely uses them as we are currently doing? It will become a mediocre animal, merely surviving as many humans are doing today.

209

Let us now examine these traits in a human being living in a tribe in nature, as he possesses all these attributes that are dormant in most of us since we are living in the system. A tribe member has to use his brain power and high consciousness to navigate a jungle that is ever changing, and has to use his logic, reason, and complex problem-solving skills at all times and in all situations. He uses science to learn about his environment—identifying hundreds of edible or poisonous plants and animals, all types of bird songs and other animal sounds in the jungle, weather patterns, and hundreds of locations, without writing one word down. He creates medicines, technologies, and builds shelters and tools. He possesses a healthy body that he uses in all types of ways as he walks, runs, jumps, climbs, and swims to provide for his tribe. He cooperates and collaborates with all the members in his tribe to achieve their common goal of survival and flourishment, and he is naturally moral, empathetic, and compassionate with the human beings that he depends on. He does not only speak his tribal language but also languages of other creatures in the jungle with him, and he is an artist that sings and dances and creates decorative and body art, clothing, and paintings. Finally, it is worthy to mention that unlike us, he is one with nature as he takes and gives back to it without polluting or destroying. So allow me to ask you some questions as we compare a member of a tribe to a human living in the system: Whose body is healthier, stronger, and more developed? Whose brain is more advanced? Who is in constant evolution and exploration? Who is more valuable to life on Earth? Who is more alive? Who is a full human being? Who is primitive and who is modern? Who is the human and who is the animal?

We have forgotten the human in us, and have reverted back to being animals because of a system that taught us that society is our true origin. We have not only been uprooted from the universe, Earth, and life, but also from who we are as human beings. We are unbelievable creatures that are living in a truly magical reality, but we are wasting our lives by devolving back to being simple animals. By doing so, we blindly destroy everything around us as we are only concerned with our own lives. The way we are living is completely unnatural, which means we are diseased as we have deviated from our nature. You must heal yourself by reconnecting to your true origins as a living entity belonging to the universe, a life form connected to all life on Earth, and finally to the human traits that separate you from other animals. Grounded and armed with this knowledge, you can now enter society and see who you can become.

I urge you to comprehend the following statement very carefully. You have the capability to be a hundred or a thousand times more human than the tribe member I mentioned above and you can do so by using the computer

211

that you have in your hand. At any moment and in any place you could be learning about these human traits and how to take action to develop them in yourself. A tribe member can get information from his jungle but knows nothing outside of it. You can learn about all the jungles on Earth and go visit them if you wish to do so, and you can learn about the whole universe including the past of humanity and all of life on the planet. If you want to enhance the artist in you, there are thousands of artists online that can inspire you and teach you. If you want to be more moral, empathetic, and compassionate, there are thousands of people on your phone waiting for you. If you want the strongest body in the world, you have thousands of videos and articles to help you get there. If you want to speak another language, there are hundreds of languages at your disposal, accessible from the mobile you look at hundreds of times every day. Use technology in a useful way to explore and learn about the world – where you have the power to be anyone you want to be. Any human trait that you choose to develop is right there for you but you must take actions to start the learning process.

Please understand that the computer in your hand that can make you as human as you can be can also make you as much of a simple animal as you can be. It is all up to what icons you choose to press on. When using the computer, TV, and other technologies, we have to beware of

212

their power to devolve us into an ordinary animal. We are physically and mentally downgrading ourselves with the misuse of these technologies. Instead of wasting the technology to follow fake TV shows, we must explore and explode our unique human potential.

The system and religion have mentally uprooted us from nature but physically we still belong 100% to it. It is imperative that we refocus on connecting our mental state back into what is absolutely and undoubtedly true. We have to stop ignoring the truth that is staring us in the face with every breath we take, every step we walk, every drop of water we drink, and every piece of food that we eat. We need to escape from the mirage that is society and reopen our eyes to a universe 13.8 billion years into its evolution, which without nothing exists. We must replant ourselves in nature, because outside of it, we are dying as we are severed from our origins.

Ask yourself all the questions that are worth asking. With diligence, the answers are at the tips of your fingers. Follow the truth where it leads you, and let it destroy the false beliefs that you did not come up with, but rather have been programmed into you from birth by society and religion. You will find that the truth has so much evidence validating it, and the beliefs that you have held onto all your life have no proof or evidence that they are at all true or valuable to who you are.

The system makes you unhealthy, unhappy, stressed, and forces you to pay for water, food, and, if possible, you will soon be charged for the air that you breathe, while the universe has given you everything for free, including the most advanced brain and body in the history of all life on Earth. The system strips you from what makes you human and downgrades you into a mediocre animal, while the universe offers you truly exceptional human traits for you to explore. The system makes your brain and body tired and diseased because of the low quality water, food and air, and fills you with false information, chemicals, pills, alcohol, and smoke, while the universe has given you sunlight that makes you stronger, fresh air, pure water, and all the healthy food you want for free. The system pollutes the air and water, degrades the soil, destroys nature, and kills species after species, while the universe keeps giving, creating, remedying, cleaning and purifying. The system imprisons you in an imaginary world locked between four walls going through the same old tired routines, while the universe tells you come travel in me, see the beauty I created for you on your planet, learn about yourself and all the life forms around you, get lost in my limitless galaxies and all that they contain, be free and dream in reality, and let your imagination run wild in the truth not the falsehood. The system says pay me and die a slow death while killing everything around you, while the universe tells you to live

214

and let live. The system is saying come and get lost, dazed, and confused in me and live in a corner of your imagination, while the universe is telling you come be free in who you are and be limitless in my truth. The system cuts down trees to make money to enslave you under, while the universe creates more and more trees that gives you oxygen and tells you, go ahead live freely, its all yours and I want nothing in return. We can keep going on and on, comparing the two, and the truth will always win over the falsehood.

Restart

Your brain and body are malfunctioning, and you must press the restart button. To restart your system, you have to go back to your origin, and as your system reboots, you must actively stay away from the psychological viruses of society that are ready to cling back on and pull you down. Focus on taking in the true information while staying away from the false information. It is important to note that you must experience the truth for yourself in order to adopt it into your life, therefore, I urge you to take action and experience what I advise you to do in this final section. Challenge the truth in my statements and adopt the ones you cannot refute, but be patient. It will take a while to rewire your brain with the truth as it has been absorbing false information for so many years. It will also take discipline, focus, sacrifice, and diligence to accomplish any worthwhile goal in life. Try this method and see what happens, what do you have to lose in seeking the truth? If it makes you better so be it, continue, and if not go back to how you were before, but give it a real effort for a few months and see what happens. Let us restart!

Most of us work five days a week for eight hours a day, spend one hour commuting to and from work, and sleep for eight hours, which leaves you with seven hours to do as you wish each day. On the weekend I imagine that you have at least 20 hours of free time. So, you have 55 hours of free time for yourself per week. Now, ask yourself what am I doing during these 55 hours per week? Can I eliminate the time spent with the false information on my television and phone and do something significant for myself instead? You do not lack the free time or the capability to revolutionize yourself. Your innate self is actually what is dying to get out and be free, and is not happy when it is locked away behind the confines of society.

Start by taking your focus off everything present in the four walls. Everything that's happening in human society between the buildings and the streets needs to be put aside. Society is nothing but a speck in the reality that you are a part of, and it has nothing to do with your true origins. Turn your attention towards the natural world that has been around for 13.8 billion years. The fact that you belong to nature is the simplest and most undisputable truth, but you have been made to believe that your existence is limited to the four walls. However you define the reality you live in, and your existence is 13.8 billion times more significant than those four walls. You must start living in the universe and on Earth as a life form, and then enter society when you need it, not the other way around. After you finish your job, do not go sit between four walls and waste your life on the screens full of meaningless distractions.

Go spend time reconnecting with nature and get out of yourself; try your best not to listen to the inner monologue that is always running through your mind. Observe the sky, clouds, sun, trees, grass, birds, animals, and listen to the sounds of nature. To be truly free, pleasant, and engaged, focus on the life forms around you, relax and take it all in second by second, minute by minute. As you get lost watching a fake TV show, do the same with the life in front of you. Sit under a tree and realize its importance for all of life on the planet including yours. Observe insects and consider their value in nature and how if it were not for then, you would not be here. Bask in the sun light and grasp that, without the sun, nothing exists on this planet. Sit by a stream of water or a waterfall and take in the fact that, without water, you and everything else on this planet would not be here. Learn about the animals and the plants and realize that without them you would have nothing to eat. Get inspired by

217

these amazing creatures, how they live their lives, and how hard they work to survive. Learn about how phenomenally intelligent they are, and their abilities can be magical in many ways. We may be higher up the food chain, but we are all equally important. There is 3.8 billion years of life around you, that you can be inspired by and learn from. Where do you think you will gain more, by sitting at home watching a meaningless show or by sitting outside in nature taking in all that it freely gives you from sunlight, fresh air, and a peaceful state of mind?

Every minute spent away from social media, imaginary video games, streaming entertainment and the world of negative news, can be a minute gained in the freedom of the universe. 99% of the information that your brain absorbs must be factual, while 1% can be imaginary and not the opposite. It is just like junk food, you eat it every now and then, but if you eat it every day for breakfast, lunch, and dinner, what do you think is going to happen to you? Same goes for the imaginary world that is destroying your psyche. Replace the damaging shows with documentaries about science, the universe, the history of life on Earth, human evolution, your brain and body, philosophy, and the unique human traits you possess. Learn the true facts about our world and start learning how you can reduce your negative impact on your brain and body, and on the life that you share this planet with. Learn about the history of humanity through paleontology, anthropology and archeology, and see the brilliance of our species in how we constructed communities, architectures, and civilizations. You can also learn from hundreds of books and documentaries about the heroes of humanity that have advanced our species forward by fighting against the system's oppression and injustice. Learn from the geniuses of humanity that have done so much good for us and follow their footsteps. Take notice that all the heroes of our species have been people fighting for human rights that have been taken from us by the heads of the system. Observe how the scientists, philosophers, environmentalists, and humanitarians are the ones who have added to the common good. With all that you take in, analyze the faults of humanity and work on reducing it within you, and find the good and inspiring in us, and develop it in yourself. All that I am telling you to do is to press on the true icons on your screens. Get the correct information and move away from pressing on the imaginary icons with their false information. It is that simple.

Please contemplate this thought carefully: all doors that have been opened for you in your life are due to other human beings opening them for you. Start with your family raising you, consider the social bonds you developed with friends in your neighborhood, fellow students in your school, and the teachers that shaped your knowledge of the world

219

both in school and university. The job that you have, the house that you live in, the technology you use, and the food and water that you drink have all been given to you by other human beings. Every single door in your life has been opened for you by another person. Therefore, if you want to move forward in your life, achieve more, be happier, realize your dreams, and have more doors opened for you in your life—you must thrive to meet new human beings and build solid, authentic, and genuine relationships to lift each other. You must develop a sense of compassion and empathy, and gain the social bonding skills to bring others into your life. Ask yourself, when was the last time you made a new friend? Why do you only have just a few friends that you have had for years? The reason is that you have replaced the need to have real relationships with real people that make a real difference in your life with imaginary friends on your screens. From your thousands of imaginary friends that you have on Facebook, Instagram, and other useless applications, to the imaginary people you get false information from in your movies and series sitting alone between four walls, you have replaced real human beings that can open real doors for you with imaginary ones that are shutting doors and locking you in.

It really needs to be understood that your brain receives information about the physical world through the five senses—sight, hearing, touch, smell, and taste. The more senses are engaged, the more information your brain receives, and the fuller and more enhanced your experience will be. Notice that most of your senses are employed when you interact with anything that is alive. For example, when you are with another human being, you can use four or five senses, in addition, you can fully interact with them as you converse and share thoughts and emotions. Please realize that you only use one or two senses with the people on your screen, and they only talk to you, but you cannot talk or interact with them in any real way. Would you rather have rich, meaningful, and fulfilling experiences with real people in real life, or dull, empty, and superficial ones with the fake people on your screen?

Stop watching these actors, and only use your phone applications to connect with your real friends and to find new people that you can meet in real life. Think about the real friends you have and how valuable they have been in your life, and work on expanding your circle of friends to include other human beings that can become as valuable to you as the people that are in your life now. You have to spend as much time as possible with your friends while you take part in different activities: Focus on sharing, laughing, thinking, planning, exercising, exploring new things that are good for you, going on adventures, and advancing together. Notice that you are the most alive when you are with the people you cherish and not when you are alone. Go out in this world, meet real human beings, and form as many real bonds as you can, and see your life explode in the best ways possible.

Get to know your body and learn about how it functions optimally. You have forgotten that you live in your body which is a fantastic piece of evolution that took millions of years to get to the state it is in. Yet, you think you live in your head as if it is not connected to your body that you have been neglecting and poisoning in so many different ways with addictive and damaging information, junk food, chemicals, tobacco, and alcohol that the people running the system are more than happy to provide you with. Taking care of your body is the most basic requirement of your life, but the majority of people refuse to do even the bare minimum. The human body is able to run marathons and climb the highest mountains, yet you use it to get you from a bed to a chair.

Your body never stops working to maintain the biological processes in you that keep you alive. In addition, it is constantly fighting to keep you healthy as it is always trying to kill germs, microbes, viruses, carcinogens, and unwanted foreign elements that enter your body. Your body requires energy to be able to perform these vital functions. You can easily see that the more you give your body bad nutrition and false information, the more it needs to fight, and the more energy it needs. This energy has to come from somewhere and it will take it from other functions that are not as important such as moving around, focusing, thinking, etc. You are running on low battery power at all times, which makes the drive to achieve important tasks and goals in your life diminish. This will make you both mentally and physically drained, lazy, less enthusiastic, and only interested in sitting or lying down. If you give your body the correct amount of water, healthy food, clean air, and true information, you will now have sufficient energy that your body can transfer to all areas in your life. You will then feel brighter, happier, more focused and active, and you will be able to accomplish all your tasks with ease.

Look at your hands, legs, stomach, chest and head— do you not wonder about how they work? We have unlimited documentaries and articles online from credible science educators teaching you everything you want to know. There are billions of things happening in your body without you noticing, and it is an unbelievable machine that is freely delivered to you by biological evolution. We understand very well about how the body works and what it needs to function optimally, but you need to dedicate time and effort to give it what it requires. Start by letting your body be exposed to sunlight 10-15 minutes every day and see your health transform. Learn about the foods you need to eat, the amount of water you need to drink, and the breathing exercises to open up your lungs capacity so it can absorb the most amount of oxygen to distribute to your body and brain. We know so many types of exercises that you can do to strengthen your body and help it stay healthy. But yet most of us do not even think to learn about the basic and most important element of our existence. We seem to want to make ourselves believe that we live outside of our bodies, and unfortunately we are succeeding in doing so while drowning in our imagination.

The brain and consciousness that a human being possesses are the most advanced of all the life forms that exist today and that have ever existed in the 3.8 billion years of life on Earth. We have used our brains and consciousness to get to the moon and take a stroll on it—has any other creature in the history of Earth been able to achieve such a feat? Do you understand how sophisticated your smart phone and other technologies are, and that the brain that created them is so much more complex? However, today, an average person is not conscious of any of these things, but rather is only conscious of minimal things which are not worthy of the most advance consciousness in the history of life. We are conscious of four or five things, which are work, a few relationships, social media, TV, and ourselves. However, we have the capability to be conscious of hundreds, thousands, millions, and billions of things in this universe.

Involve yourself in ways to upgrade your brain by learning new skills and enhancing the human in you. All the interests that you have been putting aside such as playing a musical instrument, learning a new language, reading, writing, playing a new sport, dancing, swimming, hiking, drawing, painting, creating, designing, building, and countless other challenging and beneficial activities can enhance your brain rather than keeping it dormant. Mastering the skills you are interested in will make your brain much more aware, and that will translate to all areas in your life. Your brain is like a computer and you can update and upgrade it in so many ways. If you learn a new language for example, your brain becomes more efficient and your memory much stronger. This will help you think better and be more aware in all aspects of your life as you are building new neurological connections. Furthermore, you will be able to communicate with people from a whole new culture that have a different way of thinking than yours that you can learn from, and thus you open a new door in the world for yourself.

Train your brain how to think logically, reasonably, and morally and how you can utilize the critical thinking power it possesses to discern truth from falsehood and enhance your life. Learn meditation techniques to quiet your mental state and give it a rest from the thoughts of past and future outcomes that stress you out and fill you with negativity. You have to quiet the non-stop chatter that is keeping you on edge so you can focus and start thinking clearly. I do not know why there is a lot of stigma attached to meditation, when all you are doing is closing your eyes and giving your brain a much needed rest from being bombarded by an endless stream of thoughts and stimuli from society. Do you see anything wrong with that? Plenty of scientific studies have been done on meditation and have clearly shown that it has so many benefits such as stress reduction, enhancing self-awareness, controlling anxiety, lengthening attention span, and promoting emotional health.

At the end of the day, the more you learn and do valuable things the better your brain will function, rather than doing the same things every day that keep your brain stagnant. Stop living in the imaginary world on your screens and wasting your brain power while you dissociate from reality. The movies, series, and social media do not upgrade your brain but rather confuse it, as you place it in an unrealistic world. The imaginary world on your screens doesn't teach you anything factual or valuable about human beings, but rather leaves you with fake and exaggerated information moving you further and further from real human interactions.

Realize how unbelievably lucky you are to be born in a day and age where technology and medicine have come together beautifully to open up the door for you to really learn about who you call "myself." You can go further and see how your body is connected to all of life, the Earth, the sun, and the entire universe. If you make an effort to learn about your body, brain and consciousness that arises from it, and start applying the teachings that are beneficial for your system, do you think that will make you function better or worse? Do you think you will be healthier or sicker? Do you think you will be happier or more depressed? Do you feel that you would be stronger or weaker, more lazy or more energetic? Pursuing this path would you be getting closer to your goals or further away from them?

Please keep reminding yourself that you are a life form which means you belong to life and the living creatures in it. When you drink water sometimes, think about where it's coming from and how lucky you are to have it. When you eat food, focus on what is in front of you and appreciate that these life forms are keeping you alive. Catch yourself sometimes breathing, and contemplate where this air comes from and how your body freely reacts to it. Take a moment to notice that when you are sitting alone between your four walls you are the only life form present there while you're surrounded by lifeless objects. Do you think that a life form detached from life is happy or healthy? Can you think of any other organism on Earth that isolates in such a manner that in some days it has no real contact with other life forms? You are a living being that has been severed from life by society, and you must come back to being with other living organisms. The more you spend time with anything that is alive, the more rooted to life you will be.

Travel in your city, country, or around the world and explore the natural beauty of this planet that you live on and connect yourself to life and all the wonderful species that are here with you. And if you can help another life form to live a better life, you would be truly significant to life itself. You can join countless humanitarian or environmental organizations that are helping human beings and all kinds of creatures in this world. As you give a helping hand, you will meet incredible human beings that are selfless, authentic and kind, and you can build life lasting friendships with them. At the same time, you will be contributing to saving lives which will fill you with a sense of joy, significance, and nobility. Do you not think this is better than sitting with your TV and phone, locked alone with lifeless objects between four walls? Do you not think it is better to save lives than continuing to kill blindly? Do you not want another life form to save your life if you need saving?

The simplest concept to keep in mind is that a small contribution is always better than none at all. The easiest way to begin involves simply making a conscious effort to learn how to reduce your impact on environmental degradation and global warming. For example, planting a few trees every year can be an invaluable contribution to so many life forms on our planet. Picking up a piece of plastic you see on the ground may prevent it from reaching the ocean and not only save the life of a marine animal, but inspire another person who sees you to do the same. Other examples include turning off running water while washing dishes or brushing your teeth, taking shorter showers, using less plastic products and recycling, turning off unused electrical appliances or lights, and becoming more conscious of your carbon footprint. These efforts will soon become habits, and over a lifetime, will amount to something rather than nothing.

Keep reminding yourself that the body you're in, the air, water, and food you consume, the Earth that you walk on, and every atom that composes you that come from our universe are all products of the truth. The true world is so obvious and is right there for you to explore. Connect to your body and then you will clearly see what your body is connected to. Get out of your imaginary constructed reality that only exists in a small corner of your mental process and be born again in a universe 13.8 billion years into its evolution. The true reality is so basic and plain to see that it's almost silly to point out. However, we have missed it by being born and raised with religion and the monetary system that have hypnotized us and plugged us into their imaginary world from birth. Come back to the real world which is the most objective and undeniable truth that exists.

We truly are a remarkable species, yet the psychological diseases of religion and monetary greed drive us towards extinction. These societal constructs separate us from each other, give us a self-centered perspective, and prevent our brains from reaching their incredible potential, limiting them to primitive and animalistic drives. This way of life suppresses the human characteristics that truly makes us proud to be members of this great species. We must find the strength to take a hard look at ourselves, face up to the beliefs that we hold, and question their authenticity. Then, and only then, will we be able to unlock the true potential of who we are and begin the path to becoming human.

Conclusion

Most people hear the truth every day, nod their heads, and do not change a thing in their lives. If the truth knocks on their door, they open the door just a little bit, see who is there, smile, say no thanks, and then shut the door. When the correct action should be to kick the door open, bring an axe and chop up the whole door, invite the truth into your home, take the wood to the back yard, light a fire with it, and dance with the truth as it has brought goodness into your life. The truth is knocking on your door at every moment; it is in the body you are in, the human traits you possess, the air that you breathe, the life forms that you eat, the water that you drink, the life on Earth, the moon, the sun, the stars, and the entire universe.

When you lift the vale, you will realize that you belong to something unbelievable but absolutely true. You will dive into the real world that our technological wonders have been able to bring to us on our screens right in front of us to learn about. Start with your body, the Earth, the creatures on it, humanity and its evolution, the sun, the planets in our solar system, and then expand into the limitless universe full with breath taking phenomena. Comprehend that you are apart of something so incredible that you cannot concoct in your wildest imagination, however, it's all real. Bask in the awe and wonder in the unlimited information we possess about reality that can enhance who you are as you are learning about the truth and aligning yourself with it. And then, leave your four walls and go spend time with life.

We can do so many things to enhance ourselves and the life around us. We just have to start learning the factual information about our existence, eliminate the wrong information, and follow the road of the truth with our actions. Please know its one thing to read, listen, watch, and talk. It's a whole other thing to take action. You have to learn and do, rather than learn and forget, ignore, or simply pass by and continue the same actions you have been stuck doing for years. The only way for you to take this journey is by being involved with the truth. Realize and accept the fact that you are the most complex life form on this planet, possessing the highest consciousness, and see what you can do with this gift rather than wasting it away. All the tools to transform your life are at your disposal. Make your brain and body strong; enhance your human traits, plant yourself back into life on Earth and the universe you have been uprooted from, and the truth will open up the world for you.

It is plain to see that if you belong to the system then you will inherit the qualities of the primitive animals that are running it. Knowingly or unknowingly you will be isolated from life, and you will become selfish, destructive, wasteful, neglectful, apathetic, lazy, unhealthy, full of stress and negative feelings, and blinded from seeing the truth. In contrast, if you belong to the objective truth, then you will inherit the universe and what it has freely given you: all the galaxies and the stars they contain, the sun, the Earth and the life on it, the air that you breathe, the water that you drink, the food that you eat, and the most sophisticated body and brain in the history of all life on Earth. You will then be worthy to be called a human being and you will naturally be strong, healthy, joyful, empathetic, intelligent, peaceful, giving, an advocate for all of life—and a warrior of the truth that is fighting to help all beings that are suffocating and suffering in the falsehood that is the system. So please tell me, who do you want to be?

Afterword

I would like to conclude this book by sharing a vision that I have been living on my own for many years now, but I am confident that many others share this outlook. I would like to offer an invitation to further develop this vision to those of you reading this book. Allow me to introduce a brief overview of the central concepts.

I have just succeeded in establishing a non-governmental organization (NGO) in Thailand, and in the future if possible, I would love to export the concept to other countries around the world. This foundation is comprised of a community that shows concern for the world and its inhabitants. The group's core objective is to connect passionate, open-minded, and respectful individuals to motivate, inspire, and elevate one another as well as those around them.

The foundation seeks to unite individuals from all walks of life to create an assembly that serves communities in need and makes a positive impact in the lives of children around the world. Ideally, a core group of participants will collaborate with local community members to set up a framework for volunteers to accomplish the goals of the NGO: to provide children with the necessary tools to live happy, creative, and productive lives; to implement educational programs including English, science, art, nutrition, environmental protection, physical education, and critical thinking in order to give the children and their communities the confidence to grow, and help to instill values such as morality, kindness, and altruism within them. I have worked with children in a variety of schools and foundations around the world in the last eight years, and can tell you firsthand that the majority of organizations lack this type of focus within their programs, especially in rural and impoverished communities.

The members of the organization shall be carefully selected, as they will be expected to rely on each other, form everlasting relationships, and support one another across all regions of the world. My dream includes building a network of individuals who can depend on one another's skills to improve their lives as well as the lives of those around them. This is not a foundation in which volunteers lose contact with each other after returning home; in fact, the NGO's mission involves setting up programs and activities for the children it serves, as well as the volunteers of the foundation. It is critical for the volunteers to develop friendships, have fun, and explore the culture and geography of the country in which they volunteer. I aim to connect with volunteers who are respectful, driven, and willing to cooperate for the good of the collective, to ensure everyone has an amazing experience, full of productivity and positivity.

Society has done a remarkable job of separating us from nature and from each other; however, we cannot achieve our full potential without support, guidance, and inspiration from others. As our species evolved roughly 200,000 years ago, our ability to form complex social bonds proved to be a unique characteristic crucial to our survival and evolution. I now call for the creation of a modern tribe based on collaboration, trust, and the well-being of the collective as well as the world at large.

If you would like to be a part of this foundation and want to volunteer or donate, or if you have any inquiries or comments about this book, feel free to contact me at uprooted02@gmail.com

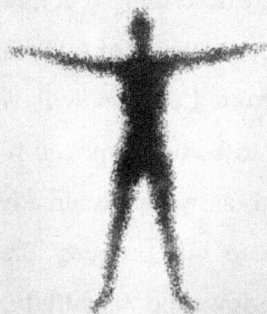

SUPERNOVA

Supernova

I have come to understand that writing about my life will allow others to gain a sense of who I am in order to better connect with my message. Though I prefer that this book's focus remain on the material I have discussed, I know that these experiences have shaped who I am and how I view the world. I want to make it clear that although I had a difficult journey to get to where I am in life today, I feel an immense sense of gratitude for what I have accomplished from the understanding that many others have endured far worse circumstances.

I shall begin by describing several of my experiences from the war; however, none of my family, friends, or anyone I have met from Lebanon will voluntarily discuss those times. It seems to be an unspoken rule that the war is not to be remembered, as we have already endured enough anguish and damage to our property, health, and mental state. Despite the sorrow and negativity, the majority of Lebanese people who survived the war now have a positive outlook and work tirelessly to achieve their dreams. I strive to live on for those who did not survive, and make a difference in the world by helping the oppressed in their honor.

The War

The Lebanese Civil War came about as a direct result of the enormous change that occurred in the Middle East with the establishment of the State of Israel. The 1948 declaration displaced hundreds of thousands of Palestinians to Lebanon and other Arab countries to make way for the incoming Jewish populations. A similar migration occurred in 1967, as a result of the six-day war with the Arab countries of Egypt, Syria, and Jordan on one side, and Israel on the other. These two relocations altered the demographic of the Lebanese population, leading to escalated tensions between Christians and Muslims, who differed greatly on how to deal with the Palestinian crisis.

Against the backdrop of Israel's consecutive defeats, clashes were taking place in Lebanon between Palestinians and the Phalanges, a Christian militia. In the early morning hours of April 13, 1975, a skirmish erupted between several guerillas from the Palestine Liberation Organization (PLO) and the Phalangist Kataeb Regulatory Forces (KRF), resulting in the accidental death of a driver for the PLO. This attack occurred outside the Church of Notre Dame de la Deliverance in Beirut while a baptism was taking place, and as the crowd exited the church an hour later, a group of unidentified gunmen opened fire, killing four KRF supporters. Believing this was a retaliation against the previous violence, Phalange militias took to the streets of

241

eastern Beirut and constructed roadblocks in many of the Christian-populated areas. A bus of PLO supporters returning from a political rally in Tel el-Zaatar unknowingly entered one of these checkpoints, and a group of Phalange militiamen opened fire, killing 27 individuals and wounding 19 others. This highly controversial incident ignited the Lebanese Civil War and resulted in the death of 300 individuals in just the first three days of fighting, and caused an estimated 250,000 fatalities in total.

At the request of Christian militias, Syrian troops entered Lebanon in June 1976 to aid the Christians against the Palestinians and their Lebanese Muslim allies. After causing considerable damage to the Palestinian military and their supporting forces, the Arab League compelled Syria to accept a ceasefire and gave the country a subsidized peacekeeping role. By July 1978, Syria could see that the Palestinian forces and their Muslim allies had begun to lose their grip on Lebanon, and taking this opportunity to advance their own political position, Syria began bombing the Christian areas they had previously supported. The war continued, as did endless suffering for both Lebanese and Palestinian populations.

With the Syrian presence in Lebanon, Palestinian forces steadily grew stronger, and their operations along the Lebanese-Israeli border became a true menace to northern Israel, where repeated cross-border attacks led to numerous casualties on both sides. The Palestinian attempt on the life of the Israeli ambassador in the United Kingdom marked a breaking point, and it became clear that an Israeli invasion of Lebanon was inevitable.

The attack began on June 6, 1982, and Israeli forces soon arrived in the capital city of Beirut, pushing the Palestinian forces into northern Lebanon. By supporting a pro-Israeli Christian president who was a strong leader in the Lebanese Christian Maronite forces, Israel hoped to sign a peace treaty with Lebanon, but the assassination of the newly-elected president caused the hope of many to quickly fade. The Israeli invasion of Lebanon sparked the creation of many resistance movements, primarily Hezbollah—the Iranian-backed group that later became Israel's most feared and resilient adversary. After the Israeli withdrawal to the South Lebanon Security Belt, the civil war continued more ferociously than ever, especially after Syria shifted allegiances once again, and sought to destroy the Palestinian forces it once fought for, using their own military as well as Lebanese Muslim groups such as the Shia Muslim Amal Movement to take control of Lebanon.

After numerous defeats, Christian militias consolidated in the Mount Lebanon region, but internal conflicts left the door open for Syria to settle the score with their Christian former allies. In October 1990, Syria occupied the Christian areas of Lebanon, ending the long civil war and placing the country under Syrian rule for the next 15 years. After more than a decade of military resistance, Lebanon liberated its southern territories occupied by Israel in May 2000. Two months after the assassination of former Lebanese Prime Minister Rafik Hariri in April 2006, Syrian troops fully withdrew from Lebanon following unprecedented peaceful protests in Beirut.

Memories of War

I was born in 1984 during the conflict in Beirut to my mother and father, the real heroes of this story, who protected my brothers and me from the madness of war. As I began to open my eyes to the world, I found myself surrounded by chaos, death, and screaming. Though I cannot recall, I remain certain that I have been crying since the day I was born due to the sound of constant explosions. No ordinary child exposed to such a clamor would react any other way; fear ruled our lives and there was no escape or respite.

During the war, the essentials we relied upon—bread, water, electricity, and gas—became extremely scarce. On many early mornings, my mother risked her life to stand in line at the bakery, and every three days, we waited at the nearest water company to fill our gallon vessels, since running water had been cut off at home. In the winter, we heated water on the stove to bathe.

A Syrian army base—with canons, missile launchers, tanks, and plenty of soldiers —was only a five-minute walk from our home in Beirut, so you can imagine the commotion we experienced as they fired and received fire from heavy weaponry. We lived on the ground floor of a six-story building, so when the fighting broke out, all of our neighbors ran down to hide in our apartment, dressed in whatever it was they had on—underwear, robes, or pajamas. Other times, our ground floor location offered wounded soldiers and civilians alike respite from the fighting as they clung to life.

We spent endless nights by candle or lantern light trying to cope with the darkness in our lives. On many occasions, bombs awoke us and we had to run into the kitchen, the safest room in our home, and this became one of my most vivid memories. My parents used to instruct my brothers and me to squat behind the door of the kitchen, thinking this would make us feel safer, but it made no difference at all. I remember the flashes of lights and the sounds of breaking glass that accompanied the blasts as our lives were plunged into complete darkness.

On one occasion, my mother spoke of meeting her brother at the boundary between East and West Beirut, as the war had divided the city. A family friend drove her and my

245

older brother to bring a tank of gas to my uncle in exchange for flour. As they approached the border, a fight broke out and a crossfire of bullets forced them to stop the car on the side of the road and hide under it during the 30-minute battle. Several weeks later, the family friend who had driven my mother and brother disappeared, and we eventually found out that he had been executed at a roadblock. Lebanese identification cards indicate religion, so if you happened to be a Christian at a Muslim checkpoint, you were killed on the spot, and vice versa.

My father once told me of a terrifying battle that broke out at a roadblock inspection. Without warning, the officer checking my father's papers instructed my father to quickly exit his vehicle and follow him to a hole in the ground, where he laid down and covered his ears as the soldier fired his weapon. I cannot imagine what that must have felt like for my father, nor do I wish to.

I vividly recall my mother purchasing a fishbowl for my brothers and me, but many mornings we woke to find the colorful fish floating on the surface of the water—the sounds of the previous night's blasts caused their heads to explode. My mother continuously replaced the fish, but after a while, the glass began cracking from the blasts. My father repeatedly glued it together until one day the fishbowl completely shattered and we never had fish again.

Nowhere is Safe

Every now and then, my mother took my brothers and me to visit her aunt across town, but the walk to her house was littered with mines set up in tight rows placed to prevent tanks from passing. Each time we prepared to travel, my mother would warn us not to walk in the middle of the street or else she would beat us. However, my brothers and I never listened—we always walked a zigzag through the mines. During the perilous trek, my mother remained silent to avoid inadvertently distracting us, but the moment we cleared the mines, she screamed at us and delivered on her threat. We ran to our aunt's house, simultaneously crying and laughing, unaware of how dangerous those objects were, though today I understand the combination of fear and anger my mother must have felt on those journeys.

Our family owned a house in the mountains of Lebanon that we returned to every so often to make sure that it had not been destroyed by constant skirmishes. Watching gunfights through the back window of the car was unforgettable—I recall seeing many cars abandoned on the side of the road as my father sped past the flying bullets. My brothers and I naively discussed how the next time we ought to jump out in order to steal the cars that had been left running as drivers fled the horror.

On one occasion, as a skirmish began near our mountain home, our family fled to a nearby basement that provided a safe haven for the neighbors whenever the attacks began. The fear was palpable in that basement, and memory of that afternoon haunts me to this day. When we returned to our house, shrapnel had shattered the windows and left bullet holes in the walls. A cannon shell had fallen right in front of our house—if we had not escaped to our neighbor's home, you would not be reading these words right now.

During the day, I shared the favorite pastime of my older brothers—collecting bullets, shrapnel, and missile propellers from the abandoned battle zones. I now realize the grave danger of this hobby, since mines or undetonated bombs could have instantly killed any one of us. By night, we watched the opposing armies shooting red and yellow tracers into the sky over our village. Amazed by their brilliant colors, I thought them beautiful, though I did not yet know what they were capable of.

The Tears Run Dry

I used to cry a lot during those days, and understandably so, yet I also remember that at a certain point, I stopped shedding tears. As the years went by and I became an adult, I found that I had become desensitized to the trauma and could not remember any of the times I had cried. When I reflected on when and how I became this way, I found myself reliving a memory from when I was six years old. I was riding in the backseat of the car with my brother, and my father was driving us to school with my mother in the passenger seat. As we traveled, I saw one of my best friends and his brother in the neighboring car, also being driven to school by their parents. My brother and I waved to them and they returned our greeting. I remember a sense of excitement as my friend's car passed ahead, and I was eager to meet at school to discuss our fortunate coincidence.

A few moments later, I could see that the police had stopped the traffic in our direction, leaving our car in the third row and our friends in the first. Suddenly, I heard the unmistakable sound of a projectile, which turned out to be two missiles, the first destroying a building right in front of us, and the second demolishing the first row of cars entirely. My mother shouted for us to crouch down as my father hastily turned the car around and sped home. As I realized what had happened to my friend and his family, the whistling in my ears was replaced by my own screams of panic and terror. My mother repeatedly tried to calm me, but the howls of agony seemed beyond my control. When we returned home, I ran to the side of the house, shaking and sobbing. I could not stop picturing my friend burning, and in an effort to regain control, I ordered myself to stop the tears, and it was one of the last times I ever cried.

I consider this the most traumatizing experience of those days because it was so personal. One of my best friends had been blown up in front of my eyes—how else could I react? I remember every single detail of that incident and will never forget its brutality. The empty desk where he once sat was a grim reminder of my friend, as well as of the constant danger we all faced.

Brothers in War

Growing up surrounded by violence, my brothers and I exhibited a great deal of anger and fought constantly. We did not get along most of the time and physically abused one another. In retrospect, I understand that our behavior reflected the turbulent environment in which we were raised, though at the time, the lion's share of the violence fell upon me, since I was the youngest and weakest. I must have been 10 years old when one Wednesday afternoon, my older brother grabbed my wrist, twisting and cracking it. I ran to my mother in agony, and she brought me to the hospital where a doctor put a cast on my arm. My mother told the doctor that I had fallen, and we returned home.

The next morning, I awoke full of rage, and approached my sleeping brother and began hitting him as hard as I could with the cast, infuriated that he had broken my arm. We began to struggle, and when I had nearly escaped, he grabbed my foot. I called for my other brother, asleep in the next bed, to help me. Instead, he was angered at the commotion, and pulled my other arm so forcefully that my forearm snapped straight out of the elbow socket. I ran screaming in pain to my mother, who again brought me to the hospital, where the same doctor once again put a cast on my arm. This time, my mother told him that I had lost my balance due to the first injury and fallen. For the next month and a half, I could not use either arm and my mother had to dress me, bathe me, and clean me after I went to the bathroom, and the shame of having to deal with this masked the pain of my broken arms. By the time my injuries had healed, the casts were already falling to pieces from the fighting between us.

As the civil war came to an end, another began to free southern Lebanon from the grasp of Israel. The majority of the fighting took place far from my home in Beirut, yet Israeli planes periodically flew over our capital, dropping bombs on power plants, airports, and other infrastructure, punishing innocent civilians for the war raging in the south. Our lives were plunged into darkness once again, and the horrible conflict persisted until May 2000.

Blindness

Surviving the war is just the beginning of my story, and the time has come to relay another challenging aspect of my young life. When I was seven years old, I began to notice that the blackboard in school appeared blurry. After a few months, I could no longer make out the words from the back of the classroom. The school alerted my parents that the school doctor had examined me and found nothing wrong with my eyes. My parents took me to another doctor, who echoed the opinion of the first. He claimed that I was jealous of my father and brothers who wore glasses, and that I was pretending not to see well in order to obtain my own pair. After a while, my vision worsened, and the school decided to move my desk to the front of the classroom. Although I could see better, I was very slow to read, and soon enough, I could no longer see the board at all.

In an effort to slow the vision loss, my parents took away the hand-held Tetris game that I so enjoyed. Since I leaned extremely close to the television in order to see it, I was soon prohibited from this as well, forced to sit across the room and simply listen to the programs. As if my childhood was not difficult enough, my favorite activities were now prohibited. As time elapsed, my mother began to notice that when we spoke to one another, I did not look her in the eye, but to her left. My friends and teachers soon noticed as well, and we returned to the ophthalmologist's office. After many painful tests and more than two years without a solution, let alone a diagnosis, we finally received an answer: a hereditary macular degeneration disease called Stargardt's would cause me to gradually lose my vision. This is when the crying began once more, but as I mentioned, my well of tears had long ago run dry, and it was now my mother who shed them.

I was the only person I knew with a visual impairment, and felt I was bound to stand out. The war-torn streets were not ideal places to walk for a person with perfect vision, let alone a partially-sighted individual. There were no centers to provide assistance and my school had never handled such a situation, so they did not know how to support me, and I was completely alone as my childhood friends began to alienate me. Painful as it felt at the time, I now understand it was a normal reaction for children seeking to blend in with their peers.

As my central vision deteriorated, I was forced to rely upon my peripheral vision. Consequently, when I tried to look another person in the eye, I shifted my gaze several inches to their left so that I could see them peripherally. When someone asked why I was not looking directly at them, I quickly tried to adjust so that my eyes would seem to focus on theirs, even though I could no longer see the person's face. An older student playing a joke on me unintentionally offered a solution to this dilemma. He would place his index finger in front of his face and tell me to follow it as he moved it to the right. As my eyes followed his finger, he would stop me at the point when I was looking directly at him. Although I did not feel great about this routine, it helped me train my eyes and make my problem less noticeable. However, there was no trick to use in class as the board and textbooks became more and more indecipherable.

My worst nightmare was hearing my name called to read aloud in class. I had to lower my face to the book in order to make out the words, so much so that my nose often touched the pages, eliciting giggles from the other students. I will never forget the time I brought my head down to read but could not judge the distance to the table, and banged my forehead against it, and the whole class erupted in laughter. As an adult, I do not blame them for any of these reactions, but at the time, their mocking felt unbearable. After a while, I told the student sitting next to me to whisper the words in the book that I had to read out loud to avoid this kind of embarrassment. Eventually, the teachers began skipping my turn and I stopped reading aloud in class altogether.

The school assigned a classmate to take notes from the board using carbon paper, which I later read at home with a hand-held magnifying glass. Since electricity was rarely available, this task was particularly difficult by candle or lantern light and this strain likely further degenerated my vision. One day, I went to my friend's house to deliver his carbon paper, but he told me that he no longer wished to take notes for me. I had to explain the situation to the school and once again face the embarrassment of the teacher asking for assistance from the other students. Fortunately, a kind classmate volunteered and I continued studying in this manner.

My father began taking my books to a copying center to enlarge the pages for me, which made them a bit easier to read, but I never took these copies to school to avoid the unwanted attention. The school enlarged my exam papers, but I was never given extra time to complete the tests, even though reading was an extremely slow process for me. Needless to say, I was behind in all my classes, and though my parents hired private teachers, I thought failure was inevitable because simple tasks had become such an ordeal. Due to the importance of education and cost of the private tutors, there was a great deal of pressure to succeed, and because I read so slowly, I spent the majority of my free time studying to catch up with my classmates.

I cannot recount how many times I heard my mother crying and cursing her luck for having a child like me. I often overheard her complaining to family members and friends, but after a while, embarrassment caused her to stop telling people that I had a problem, and I do not blame her because I felt the same way. She was a devout woman, and brought me to Christian healers and to many holy sites in my country, but it was incredibly awkward when priests placed their hands or oil on my eyes and mumbled religious phrases over my head. I felt pitied, and these practices did nothing but further frustrate me.

With a life full of confusion, shame, and negativity, I was bound to explode. I never shared any of the horrible events in my life, pretending instead that everything was normal so that I would not be pitied. Finally, at age 15, I reached my breaking point. In the ninth grade, students had to pass a government exam to continue studying, and though we sent a request to have the exam papers enlarged ahead of time, when the time came to take the test, I was given an exam in the standard font. There was nothing I could do about it, and I sat for hours trying to see whatever I could on the pages. I ended up failing, and the director of my school—a nun—later called me into a meeting. She bluntly told my mother and I that I would amount to nothing and should be placed in a blind center, and with that, I was kicked out of high school.

At that moment, everything in my life came crashing down. Since the day I was born, I had experienced nothing but death, anguish, misery, hatred, discrimination, pressure, and anger, which led to my first supernova at age 15. My mother said that she would place me in another school, but I refused, and that entire summer was filled with arguments, rage, and resentment. I used to slam the door and walk the streets feeling empty and numb, but finally agreed to attend school on the following conditions: I did not want to hear any more about my issue, or how badly I was doing in school. It was time for me to feel in control of my life, without the pressure to succeed from my family. I simply wished to be happy, and thus began my road to positivity. For the first time in my life, it was clear to me what I needed to do—look beyond the negative experiences and forget all the pain, while at the same time strive to remain optimistic, have as much fun as possible, and truly enjoy my life. After this realization, I no longer stopped to consider the potential consequences of my actions; I became somewhat fearless and began doing anything I felt like, no matter how irresponsible or dangerous it seemed.

I cut all ties with my old school, except for one childhood friend because he never looked at me differently and remains my best friend to this day. I am sure you can understand why I wanted nothing to do with the students and administrators who told me I could not make it. A new school provided me the opportunity to start over, though once again, I was the only student with a vision problem. However, the teachers and school director were much kinder, and aside from my classmates, the majority of students did not even know of my problem since I played on the school's basketball team.

I behaved as though nothing was wrong and never spoke about my problem with anyone. A classmate next to me read what was written on the board, and exam papers were enlarged for me, even though I was never given extra time to complete the tests. I excelled in the subjects that did not require a great deal of reading—math, physics, and biology—and earned some of the highest grades in the class. I continued to fail the exams that required a great deal of reading, often choosing instead to stare at the teacher or wall in sheer frustration at the idea of struggling for an hour to read a text that only took my classmates 15 minutes. The teachers failed me, as they should have, but the director looked the other way and continued to pass me.

I joined the school basketball team and concocted various strategies that allowed me to play to the best of my ability. I instructed my teammates to pass me the ball in a certain manner when I raised my hand so I knew to expect the pass from a particular direction, or I would dash to the three-point line, receive the pass, and cut to the basket. I could not see the rim, but could judge my distance to it, and knew I had scored by the sound of the ball swishing through the net. I spent endless hours training alone to determine the distance to the basket from my position on the court. Though I was 50% blind at this point, I became one of the best players in my school, and our team won many titles and competitions. The players on the opposing team never knew which way I would attack the basket since my eyes never looked in the direction I was headed.

Though my vision impairment turned out to be an unforeseen advantage for our basketball team, simply walking down the street remained one of my greatest challenges. The sidewalks, already littered with obstacles, had been severely damaged during the war, and the streets had no traffic lights or right-of-way rules whatsoever. Since I did not use a cane, I began to mentally map the city from holes and puddles to streets and sidewalks. I had to keep track of trees, railings, metal poles, and stairs. I strained my ears to avoid oncoming cars as I crossed the street, and in addition to the occasional stumble or fall, constantly injured myself by knocking into obstacles. My legs, feet, and toes took quite a beating, but I never complained because I was tired of people feeling sorry for me. I realized I could use the footsteps of pedestrians in front of me as a guide, a technique I continue to employ to this day to help me avoid injury.

During this time, I attempted to blend in and appear as normal as possible. I loved to play billiards and go to the movies with my friends, never mentioning my vision impairment. At the end of the school year, I passed the government exam (in large print) with flying colors. I finally felt as though I could succeed and left all pain behind, determined to enjoy life and experience joy. In my final years of high school, I did well in my classes and shined on the basketball court. I even asked a girl out and she accepted.

Everything about my life appeared normal; however, I was not—only a handful of people knew that I had lost 50% of my vision.

My Big Break

In 2002, an opportunity presented itself that I knew I needed to take advantage of. My parents' friends from the United States came to visit us in Lebanon and I spent that summer hearing how amazing America was from their son. When his parents discovered my visual impairment, they added more fuel to the fire by describing the services and assistance the United States offered for people like me. When I was born, my uncle living in America had sponsored my family for green cards. After 10 years, the paperwork came through, and I knew that I could move to the USA and begin a better life for myself with this card. Since I was 18 years old, I figured I could now become independent from my parents. I felt invincible and decided that nothing would stop me from going to America. I grew up fascinated by the great country depicted in movies, television shows, and music, and unable to rely on subtitles, I already had a firm grasp on the English language.

When I informed my parents of my plans, they refused on the grounds that I could not take care of myself, so I decided to figure things out on my own. I knew travel would require a passport, and used the money I received for my 18th birthday to obtain it. With this task accomplished, my parents knew there was no stopping me and they accepted my decision on the condition my mother would follow at a later date to assist me. Though I wanted to stand on my own two feet and prove to myself that I could move on with life, I had no choice in the matter. Nevertheless, I could not contain my excitement at the prospect of moving to America.

Virginia

Within a few days of my arrival in August of 2002, I had moved in with our family friends in Richmond, Virginia and obtained a full-time job stocking shelves and emptying the trash at a small complex consisting of a pharmacy, supermarket, and antique gallery. After a few months, I became a shelf stocker at the supermarket and a furniture delivery man at the gallery. I told my fellow employees that I had a mild vision problem and pretended to see more than I could, a skill at which I had become quite adept by that time. I was proud of myself for advancing in my first job, even though it was exhausting—the other workers often took advantage that I was the youngest and strongest guy on the team. However, I knew I had to make the best of the situation.

I had completed 11th grade in Lebanon and expected to attend another year of high school in the United States, but discovered that I had already taken all the classes needed to graduate. I was eligible to enter college, yet unable to do so since I could not see to use a computer. At the Virginia Department for the Blind and Visually Impaired, I added my name to the six-month-long waiting list for computer training. My mother arrived soon afterwards, got her own job preparing Lebanese food in a nearby deli, and we moved into an apartment together.

Attending classes at the center for the blind was a truly eye-opening experience. For the first time in my life, I was surrounded by people just like me, and I no longer felt the need to hide or pretend when I visited. I was fascinated by these incredible people and the challenges they faced, many far greater than my own. Though I felt fortunate that my vision loss was not as severe as the majority of the other students, I also came to appreciate the fact that my lack of support growing up strengthened my sense of independence. I realized that if I *had* grown up in the United States and received support initially, I would likely have lived a far more reserved and sequestered life. However, I also recognized that I needed plenty of help and I was ready to receive it.

I began educating myself in every way possible, beginning with simple tasks such as cutting my nails, a chore my mother had always done for me up until that point. I became adept at using a knife, cooking, and preparing my own food. I learned how to fold my money into different shapes to differentiate the bill denominations. I discovered a magnifying program for the computer and speech software to read the onscreen text aloud, as well as CCTV, which allowed me to magnify anything I wished to study. I learned how to operate these technologies and several basic computer programs, and within a short time, found myself mastering countless tasks that I previously thought impossible.

Finally, I learned how to properly cross the street and obtained useful tips on traffic movements from the mobility trainers. Traffic lights, sidewalks, and door-to-door transportation services for the disabled made the streets of Virginia far easier to navigate than those of Beirut. Even the public buses announced the upcoming stops and the route number when the doors opened. The mobility trainers advised me to use a cane, but I declined, even though I really did need it. After all the years I spent trying to hide my impairment, I just could not let myself be seen in that way. I am certain it partially stems from the desire that any young person feels to blend in with their peers, but I also did not wish for blindness to become part of my identity.

Since my vision would continue to deteriorate, I had previously decided to enter into a field where this would not be an issue. I found myself fascinated by biology and the human body, so I decided to enroll in a massage therapy program. The center for the blind provided me with a tape recorder for class lectures and offered to assign me a personal note-taker. For the first time in my life, I was finally receiving all the assistance I needed to succeed. The process of recording the lessons in class, re-listening to them at home, and taking my own notes under the CCTV was very labor-intensive, but I excelled thanks to my tenacity and determination to achieve my goals on my own terms. I quit my job to focus on my education, and graduated with the highest grades in my class at the massage school the following year.

Los Angeles

While I attended school in Virginia, one of my brothers moved to Los Angeles as part of his training in hotel management, and I fell in love with the city and its weather when I visited him. I decided that I would move there upon completion of my massage training, and did so in June 2004. My brother had returned to France to continue his studies, so I stayed with a friend of his for several weeks until I got a job as a massage therapist in a gym and could afford my own apartment. At the age of 20, I had finally begun my independent life in Los Angeles.

Two years later, I decided that the time had come to attend a university. Hindered by the high cost, a friend of mine suggested that I apply for a scholarship with the largest organization for the blind in America—the National Federation of the Blind (NFB). I entered an essay competition and received a phone call several months later from a representative who informed me that I had won a scholarship to attend the national convention of the NFB in Dallas, Texas. Upon arrival at the hotel where the convention was to take place, I realized that the entire building had been booked by this organization and was amazed that more than 1,500 blind individuals could independently navigate the grounds. I heard many inspiring stories and met fascinating and accomplished blind individuals including lawyers, doctors, and teachers.

At the end of this motivational weekend, I returned to Los Angeles and made plans to attend Santa Monica College (SMC), determined to do well and obtain a scholarship to a larger university. I continued working as a massage therapist in West Hollywood and took the bus to Santa Monica to attend classes. I did not know it at the time, but over the course of the next two and a half years, three classes would forever change my life.

The Big Three

The first was an Evolutionary Psychology class that caused me to lose my belief in God within one hour of the first day of the semester. Until that moment, I profoundly believed in God and often prayed before going to sleep. I remained certain that He was the explanation for my existence, and since I had never been exposed to any other information, I never questioned that belief. I had been born into the Christian religion and spent much of my childhood attending church as well as partaking in religious activities, including being an altar boy. I regularly attended bible study and Christian school until the age of 15, but when it came to studying science and biology in Lebanon, the subject of evolution had been quickly glossed over and I knew nothing of it.

But in the first hour of the first class, our professor, a knowledgeable gentleman in his sixties spoke of human origins, our evolution, and how psychology tied them all together. I already knew the value of logical scientific study, but was unaware that an entire field had been dedicated to our evolution as a species. His mention of humans having evolved from apes in Africa completely blew me away, and by the time I left, I had come to the realization that God does not exist. I felt inexplicably lighter, as though a huge weight had been lifted from my shoulders. Deep inside, I had never felt spiritual or religious, yet clung to certain ideas about the

266

world which had been imparted to me as a child. I had previously been unable to doubt God because I had been taught that it was wrong to do so and feared enraging an omnipotent being. But that first class offered a dose of factual information that I could not deny, leading me to my second supernova.

My entire view of the world had been shattered, and I was left with feelings of confusion and anger for clinging to these false ideas for such an extensive time. I no longer knew the purpose of life, where I had come from, or where I was going. I felt empty inside, and must admit that I became a nihilist. My previous belief in God had left no room for anyone to challenge my faith because I ignored anything that opposed my ideas. At the time, I believed myself more knowledgeable than everyone else, but looking back, I see that I was simply egotistic.

This experience taught me several valuable lessons: not to believe everything I had been told, the importance of investigating a claim before adopting it, and to always leave room for doubt. I spent the semester learning how our ancient brain functioned, and that our modern brain remains biologically indistinguishable from our ancestors, despite changes in the world around us. By the end of the first semester, a million unanswered questions flooded my brain. My desire for knowledge of the natural world had been ignited, and so began my quest to discover the real answers to life's questions.

The second class to drastically alter my worldview was Communications, which analyzed the many tricks advertisers and the media play on the public. The professor helped us understand the exploitation of the general public in order to sell products by dissecting cartoons, music videos, television shows, and movies. Since I wished to remove all deceptive elements from my life, I gave away my television, even though I had been watching movies and shows during most of my free time until that point. When I realized the effect the television had on my brain, I no longer wished to enjoy this form of passive entertainment. It became clear that I am part of a social species that learns about the world by listening to and observing the behaviors of their fellow human beings, yet on a typical day, I was spending more time watching television than interacting with actual people. I realized that dedicating so much time to an imaginary world as a means of making sense of reality was not only absurd, but a waste of time. I replaced my cable subscription with a Netflix account and resolved to only watch educational documentaries and stand-up comedy, which helped relieve the sense of overwhelming negativity I felt about our horrible and destructive actions toward nature and each other, exposed in the documentaries I was watching every day.

Philosophy was the third class to cause me to rethink my outlook on life. From both ancient and modern philosophers, I studied morality, ethics, justice, and how these issues affect our modern society. In this class, I began to understand the dual existence of subjective and objective world views, and I began to realize the importance of an objective reality, independent from personal beliefs. As part of the philosophy class, I took a sustainability class, where I learned more about the extent to which humans have damaged the environment. Participating in a beach clean-up gave me a first-hand account of the volume of trash that ends up in our oceans, and this was the first instance of actively reducing my destructive impact on the natural environment. I realized I was living in the most wasteful country in the world in terms of pollution and war, and that I was contributing to these processes by simply living there.

These classes and professors exposed me to a whole new world in which I was already living, but knew nothing of; and so began my search for truth through the lenses of science and philosophy. Science provided me with the logical order of the world, while philosophy shaped my outlook with the knowledge I gained through science. I wanted to learn more about anything and everything in order to understand who I was and what I was doing here. I found that one of the best places for me to learn about my fellow human beings was on the massage table. Once trust is established and clients relax, they completely open up to reveal their deepest thoughts and feelings, and even though I did not personally experience the events relayed to me, I could still learn from them. I also vicariously faced my patients' problems and tried my best to offer advice, and realized I could play a valuable and more meaningful role in helping others.

In early 2007, a dear friend notified me of the AIDS Lifecycle—a bike ride dedicated to raising funds and awareness for HIV/AIDS. I had not ridden a bicycle since age six due to my vision loss, but with my friend's support and encouragement, I agreed to begin training, and we purchased a tandem bicycle. In June 2007, my friend and I cycled the 545 miles (877 km) between San Francisco and Los Angeles. We rode roughly twelve hours a day for seven days and raised $9,000 for this wonderful cause. I became the first legally blind person to participate in the ride since its inception in 2001.

The following year, I joined the California Association of Blind Students and served a two-year term as both a board member and one of the organization's most successful fundraising chairmen. At our 2009 Detroit convention, I was awarded scholarships for academic excellence for having placed among America's top 30 blind students. I had the great honor of shaking the hand of Raymond Kurzweil, a pioneer in technological applications for the blind. As the year came to a close, so did my studies at Santa Monica College, and I was on my way to the University of Southern California (USC) with a full scholarship to study Human Performance (Exercise Science).

Awakening

During my two years at USC, I dove into various scientific classes that further opened my eyes to the rigorous methods of data collection in a lab. However, I did not enjoy learning in a university setting and realized that in the long run, it was an enormous waste of time and money. With internet access and a desire to learn, you can study anything for free from your home, and what I learned about the world on the internet far surpassed the knowledge I gained in a classroom setting.

I watched documentary after documentary and pored through scientific journals. I studied biological evolution, ecology, zoology, anthropology, paleontology, archeology, anatomy, psychology, history, and religion. I assessed the destructive impact of humanity on the environment and other species on the planet. I examined the monetary system of debt that we are all born into and are somehow expected to follow. I investigated the history of war as well as the rise and fall of vast empires. I studied the human and environmental cost of doing business with Western

271

corporations and the circumstances which deny people access to clean drinking water and food simply because they do not have money. I traced human evolution from the origin of our species through a long chain of hominids dating back roughly seven million years to the modern species we have become today. I studied our psychology and requirements for the human brain to function optimally. I listened to scientists and philosophers discuss everything under the sun, enjoying every moment of it, but still felt there was something lacking from my own story, much like the missing piece in a puzzle. The piece I needed to complete the puzzle did not exist under the sun, but instead surrounded it.

I must have been roughly 26 years old when I happened upon a documentary that focused on our universe. Before that point, I did not even have the slightest idea that it existed, and thus never thought that it had any significance in my life whatsoever. This documentary spoke about the origin and evolution of the universe, as well as how the solar system was formed. It articulated the immense size of the universe, and halfway through, I paused the video, and fell backwards onto my bed, completely overwhelmed in a moment I will never forget, having just experienced my third supernova. I felt lighter and freer with the realization that I was so insignificant compared to the enormity of the universe. It was a great relief to liberate myself from all the stresses, expectations, and social constructs that had imprisoned me my whole life. I no longer lived in a city in a country, or even on a planet; I had simply been born into a universe 13.8 billion years in its evolution. I wanted to study everything about it and find out what my role in it was. I devoured one scientific documentary after another and was completely blown away—my life would never return to what it had previously been.

I had lost my old sense of self and entered into the universal realm. The mystery of my existence had finally been solved, and I began to view the world in a whole new way. I now understood how innately connected to nature I was, owing my very existence to everything outside myself. I began to grasp the grandeur of the greater narrative to which I belonged and how amazingly beautiful and uniquely spectacular it was. I recognized how extraordinarily fortunate I was to be alive for however many years I may have. I could see that this story began long before my time and will continue long after I depart this world, which instilled a sense of urgency to utilize the limited time I have to contribute to the story of humanity.

However, it troubled me that I could not shake my own sense of insignificance in the world, and I asked myself how I could become a meaningful part of an ever-evolving universe. I saw myself as a member of one of many species on Earth and figured that the only way I could achieve significance was to actively engage in this life. I needed to make a real difference in the world for humanity, as well as the natural biological life that supports it. If I could help my species evolve in a positive direction, I thought it could also serve to protect other species of life. I knew that whatever little I could do, I would at least have made an effort to better the world. Since many problems of humanity's predicaments are resolvable, and the disconnection from our roots damages the natural world, the only way I could make an impression upon the universe would be to make a positive impact on humanity. Even if I could not achieve a far-reaching impact, I figured I would make the attempt, as I now believed that this was the singular channel to significance and greater meaning in my life. Discovering the changes that shaped our universe 13.8 billion years before I was born led me to want to become a part of that story, because no matter what anyone says, this is the *real* story that we *all* belong to. We belong to this planet, we belong to all life living upon it, and we belong to the universe.

Becoming Human

I figured that I could work toward being a significant member of life on Earth and a part of the solution to our destructive actions in one of two ways—first, by educating others with this book and talking to the individuals that I meet; and second, by directly assisting the victims of the monetary system I am a part of. I felt the greatest desire to focus my work on children born into poor families in impoverished areas of the world. I believe these children face suffering and misery for no apparent reason other than existing in the wrong place at the wrong time. I could easily relate to growing up in an unstable environment through no fault of one's own, and could not bear to stand idly by while I knew that I could help children, their families, and their communities.

I came to understand that I could do so much to improve this world for the next generation, and even if I failed, I would at least have made a positive change in humanity and life on the planet, no matter how small. I realized I could not live a more amazing life than one filled with traveling, discovering the natural beauty of the planet, learning, growing and helping others and nature, or perhaps even undo part of the damage that we have already done. I also recognized that my generation may be the last to have an opportunity to make a real change in the world, since we are slightly less immersed in and distracted by technological wonders than subsequent generations. I felt an insatiable desire to try to make a difference in any possible way, and knew that I had finally discovered how I could find significance in the universe, and a global citizen was born.

It took me three years of scientific research and philosophical self-reflection to desensitize my brain to all the incorrect and biased information I had accumulated. In order to arrive at this worldview, it took 26 years to realize that I played a role in a problem existing long before my birth. Realizing all that I did, the time had come for me to act. With the few months I had left prior to graduation, I hatched a plan to leave the United States and make a meaningful impact in the lives of others around the world.

I completed my studies in December 2011, sold everything I owned, and at age 27, returned to Lebanon to visit my family before I embarked on my mission. At the onset of this journey, I felt incredibly inspired, determined, and freed of all my problems. I had even forgotten that I was roughly 60% blind at this time, a fact I was soon reminded of while descending a staircase at my home in Lebanon. I tripped on the stairs, landing with a great deal of weight on my left ankle, and it snapped immediately. Unfortunately, the recovery for this injury delayed my trip for nearly a year. My girlfriend from Los Angeles decided to visit me in Lebanon, as well as travel and volunteer with me in Asia, and so we set off for Laos in October 2012.

In Laos, I saw how people lived in the less-developed world, and by contrast, how much happier they appeared than people enjoying luxurious lifestyles. My girlfriend suggested that we volunteer to teach English, since there was a high demand for it in the area. Though I had never given it much thought until then, I began to appreciate how English had changed my life for the better, and could be utilized as a tool to improve lives around the world. English is the number one language of communication, and the majority of technical information is written in English. If you speak English, you are more likely to earn more money as well as gain access to a greater number of job opportunities around the world. I knew that by teaching English to the children in rural villages, they would have a better chance to earn higher wages, support their families, and live a better life.

In Luang Prabang, Laos we volunteered at a local school with a program called Big Brother Mouse, where students received assistance with their homework after school. We met a man who taught English at a temple to children training to become Buddhist monks and he invited us to join him. We gladly accepted and my time at the temple was the most amazing experience of my life. We spent a month helping young children who had been sent by their impoverished families to become monks to bring honor and good fortune to their relatives. It was an incredibly humbling and eye-opening experience to interact with such peaceful and gentle people. After a month in Laos, we boarded a boat and arrived in Thailand to meet a Lebanese friend of mine who I had invited to join us. We had already contacted a high school in northern Thailand for our month-long volunteer opportunity, and the three of us headed to a small village in the middle of nowhere, nestled among mountains, rice fields, and rivers. It was a challenging, yet amazing and rewarding experience. After a month, my friend and I decided to travel a bit more throughout Asia, while my girlfriend decided to go to France. Although we parted ways, reflecting on those times fills me with appreciation for her introducing me to the village and allowing me to discover that I can have a meaningful impact as an English teacher.

After three weeks of traveling through Thailand, Cambodia, and Malaysia, my friend returned to Lebanon and I made my way to Austin, Texas to the US's best high school for the blind. During my travels in Asia, I had decided to outline the discoveries and experiences that led to my new way of thinking. I volunteered as a geometry teacher at the school for four months, during which time I took advantage of their technological assistance to research the information for this book. I also considered applying for the Peace Corps, but did not want to wait for the year-long application process, and also determined it was best not to become involved in the politics of a large organization. I decided to volunteer on my own instead, so after I finished my research, I said goodbye to my students, and left for Thailand once again. I wanted to return to the school that I initially volunteered in, live in peace, experience the village life, and begin writing.

Silent Solitude

As the only foreigner in a village surrounded by incredible mountains, rivers, and rice fields, I began to feel that my actions finally had significance. I spent my days teaching, writing, learning Thai, exercising, interacting with the community, and enjoying the pristine nature. I originally did not plan to stay in one place for long, until I saw how productive I had become. I greatly enjoyed the rapid progress of my students, as well as their delight in interacting with someone so different.

For the first six months, I lived in a wooden house that had been set aside for the teachers of the high school and slept in a small room on a very hard mattress. I decided that if I wanted to contribute to the community on a long-term basis, I needed a more comfortable house with air conditioning, since the countless mosquito bites and restless nights on a hard mattress had already taken its toll on my body. I searched for a place in the village, found the most amazing house I had ever seen, and moved in immediately. The house stood on stilts at the tree line and I was completely surrounded by nature, making it the perfect location to spend my nights writing and contemplating life.

I continued to volunteer at the high school, but decided that I needed to earn a bit of money to pay for meals and the new house, and I soon met a primary school teacher who altered the course of my stay in Thailand. Kru Wit (kru

279

means teacher in Thai) became one of the most inspirational people to enter my life and genuinely deserves a Noble Prize in Education for his dedication to his students. Though Kru Wit was in his late fifties and twice my age, he shared my outlook entirely. He ran a weekend school to help children from the surrounding villages, and even invited struggling students to learn at his home in the evenings.

It did not take him long to recognize the part I played in the village and invite me to join him, and at the end of the year, I stopped volunteering at the high school to work solely with Kru Wit. I told him that I was there to help and that beyond paying for meals and rent, money was of little importance to me, so he devised a plan in which each student would bring me roughly three dollars at the end of each month to cover expenses. He spoke to the directors of the primary schools, and over the next two years, I taught students between the ages of 10-12 in nine of the surrounding village primary schools.

Everyone in the community knew about my vision loss, but no one seemed to care or even notice. I taught at three different schools each semester, and Kru Wit arranged for the teachers to pick me up from one school and bring me to the next. The villages were not far from one another, and the enthusiastic Thai teachers recognized that a committed volunteer English teacher was certainly worth a few minutes of additional driving.

Since I was the only foreigner in the village, the families of all the students greeted me everywhere I went, treated as a valued member of the community. I experienced nothing but kindness and smiles, and my interactions with the children were the most valuable, since my mission was to help them prepare for a brighter future. I had several superstar students, including one that received a perfect score on her government exam. Another won the English speech competition in our district and went on to compete in the northern finals with two others, who won the district competitions in story-telling and singing. During a period of three years, I know I made a lasting difference in their lives, and our connection felt positive, pure, and genuinely human.

The Struggles

Throughout the rainy season, powerful lightning storms caused the electricity in the village to go out on a regular basis. I spent the nights in complete darkness watching flashes of light dance across the sky and listening to explosive blasts of thunder. These storms simultaneously provided amazing visual experiences and humbling sensations. I used to go onto the patio to watch the night sky, jumping in fear and awe as each strike illuminated the darkness. I will truly never forget those moments and the feelings I experienced during this incredible natural phenomenon. Though they were somewhat indescribable, the storms certainly instilled in me an appreciation for being alive.

During a particularly severe hail and windstorm—the likes of which I have never seen before or since—I felt certain I would die. As a storm approached the village late in the afternoon, intense winds began to blow so powerfully that the house started to sway back and forth upon its stilts. The sound of hail hurtling onto the aluminum roof was absolutely deafening and went on without respite for more than half an hour. I heard several aluminum sheets on the roof being ripped from the structure and some glass windows shattering in the relentless gusts of wind. It was truly terrifying, and the only small comfort I could find was that I would at least die while doing something positive for others. When the storm subsided and I could finally open the door, I saw hail the size of marbles covering the ground. I later learned that the hail had broken the windshields of many cars and injured several people who had been caught in the open. It was a terrifying experience, but surviving it made me feel more alive than ever.

With the onset of Thailand's dry season, the farmers in the countryside burn the remaining crop fibers to prepare the land for planting. During that time, I would have respiratory problems for at least a month, my coughing often waking me up in the middle of the night. I tried every medicine under the sun, but the cough persisted until the burning stopped. During this season, the temperature reaches 95-104°F (35-40 °C), and during one particularly sweltering period, ants filled and damaged my air conditioner. At the same time, my bed became infested with bedbugs, and since equipment repair took quite a long time in the village, I spent three sleepless weeks in the scorching heat, forced to wear socks, sweat pants, and a hooded sweater to avoid as much of the biting as possible.

Once the sun had set in my village, everyone closed their shops and went home, as did I, and over the next two and a half years, loneliness began to eat away at me. When storms knocked out the electricity, I faced my solitude in complete darkness, and the thought of my students often helped me endure many lonesome nights. After encountering these struggles, I lost the inspiration to write, believing it would not serve a purpose. I felt genuinely burned out and it was not until I left Thailand for South America that I was able to continue.

South America

I decided to continue my journey of volunteering in South America, and left Thailand in October 2016. By the end of three years, I had become fluent in Thai and its northern dialect, taught English at 11 different schools, helped thousands of children, and had written roughly 400 pages detailing my experiences in preparation for this book. I passed through Lebanon and the United States to visit friends and family, then landed in Colombia on December 4, 2016.

In Colombia, I was the only teacher and solitary foreigner volunteering with Fundación Juanfe, which assisted teenage mothers and pregnant girls. Due to limited funding, they were unable to cover my food or accommodation expenses, and since the foundation was located in a very dangerous neighborhood in Cartagena, I decided to stay in a safer part of town. I soon found myself skipping meals to cover the expense of hiring a taxi to drive me the 45 minutes each way to the foundation.

Working with these girls opened my eyes to how a lack of sex education in poor religious communities led to sex without protection, and caused a teenage pregnancy epidemic. My coworkers informed me that unwed teenage mothers have the highest percentage of infant mortality rate in Colombia, since they often lack the resources and knowledge to care for their newborn babies. I was responsible for instructing 160 girls aged 13-19, most of whom brought their babies to the classroom, making for quite a chaotic learning environment. The students seemed troubled and heavy-hearted—their pregnancies robbed them of their own childhood, and they now faced the challenges of motherhood in addition to poverty. In the two and a half months I worked for Juanfe, I put forth my best effort to lay a foundation for the students to learn English and hopefully find better employment opportunities as a result.

Next, I made my way to the rural beach town of Puerto Lopez, Ecuador, where I joined the Clara Luna Foundation, which focused on children's literacy, art projects, and protecting local beaches. The foundation offered me low-cost accommodations, but without a food allowance, I continued skipping meals. The other volunteers and I taught English to enthusiastic primary and secondary students for two and a half months, and the foundation even arranged an opportunity to assist communities that had been displaced from their homes for more than a year due to earthquakes in the area. I found the sight of entire families crammed into small plastic huts without electricity or running water truly shocking and humbling.

After my volunteer work with Clara Luna, I traveled to the Quechua village of Quilotoa, located at 13,000 feet (4,000 m) in the Andes Mountains. Hiking an extinct lagoon-filled volcano in freezing and low oxygen conditions completely alone was a perilous mission to undertake for a visually impaired person, but I returned victorious despite several brushes with danger. I had never felt more alive or physically accomplished, and it gave me the push I needed to continue on to the ancient Inca city of Cusco, Peru where I awaited the arrival of my dear friend Paola, the founder and director of the Clara Luna foundation in Ecuador. I had been reluctant to explore the ancient ruins of Machu Picchu alone, but Paola reassured me that we would do it together. I traversed treacherous paths on jagged stairways following in the footsteps of Paola and other hikers. It was a truly magical experience filled with majestic views and I was amazed at my ability to navigate this mysterious city of the Incas.

The next stop on my volunteering journey landed me in the city of Chincha, Peru to work with Bemelsa, a foundation dedicated to educating and providing meals for 130 underprivileged children from impoverished neighborhoods. Over the course of two months, another volunteer and I prepped the dining room, served breakfast and lunch to the children, and taught English in the afternoons. Grateful that Bemelsa provided me with a room, I spent the majority of my days inside the foundation walls teaching, writing, learning Spanish, and exercising. I noticed that many of the teenagers carried the heavy burdens of studying, working, and caring for younger siblings as their parents struggled to make a living.

My next volunteer experience took place in the Chilean fisherman's village of Taltal, where I and several others taught English to both children and adults with a foundation called English for the Greatest as part of the Taltal Social Project. After two months of assisting the villagers of this seaside community, I unfortunately had to cut my visit short when a child pushed me from behind while playing a game. I lost my balance and aggravated a previously torn meniscus, so I returned to Peru, where I would be better-equipped to rehabilitate my injury and continue my work with Bemelsa.

This time around, I was the only volunteer in the foundation, and facing an injury alone in a foreign land had begun to take its toll on me. I woke up one morning to a call from the director of the foundation that forever changed the course of my journey in South America—one of my 15-year-old students had hanged himself in his room. In that moment, I sensed a dark shadow creeping in as I served lunch at the funeral service. Watching the sister of the deceased cry and eat in silence was unbearable. Since breakfast, lunch, and classes had been cancelled for the following three days, I found myself all alone in the empty foundation, and the dark shadow engulfed me. I believe I experienced a nervous breakdown, and I count the next two days alone in the foundation as one of the toughest times of my life. After emerging from the darkness, I decided to end my volunteer journey—I was out of money, injured, 70% blind, and all alone. I had lost 24 pounds (11 kg) in a single year, and having sacrificed as much as I could, I realized it was time to stop for now. After traveling through Brazil, I returned home to take care of myself.

On the Road Again

After three months of rehabilitating my injured leg in Lebanon, I felt strong enough to get on the road again, returning to the rural village in Thailand where I had lived in the previous years. I figured that since I was already familiar with the area, I could maintain my independence without further injuring my leg, and in April 2018, the community warmly welcomed me back to teaching positions in both the public and weekend schools.

I have achieved an incredible amount during this eight-year span of volunteering: I worked in 17 different schools and foundations on three continents, explored 10 countries, and truly immersed myself in their cultures by learning two new languages. I have met and connected with people from all over the world, and pushed and challenged myself to reach for goals that I had previously only dreamed of achieving. I compiled some of my experiences in a video journal which can be accessed by searching "Uprooted" (YouTube Chanel) from a Google home page. Finally, I completed this book, and established a non-profit educational organization dedicated to giving children in need a brighter future.

Made in the USA
Middletown, DE
18 March 2022